THE SINS OF SOCIETY

WALMER BELLES-LETTRES

OUIDA on GREATNESS:

"It is impossible for the ordinary mind, which is usually dense of perception and greedy of observation, to attempt to measure or conceive in any degree the unsupportable torment to a sensitive temper and an exalted intelligence of the mosquito swarm of inquisitive interrogators and commentators; of the exaggeration, the misrepresentation, the offensive calumnies, and the still more offensive admiration, which are the daily penalty of all greatness. The adoring American, perched staring in the pear tree outside the dining-room window, may well have embittered to Tennyson the meats and wines of his dinner-table within. If he had got up from his table and shot the spy, such a pardonable impulse should certainly have been considered justifiable homicide..."

OUIDA on CHRISTIANITY:

"How is it to be accounted for – this impotence of Christianity to affect the policies, politics, legislation and general life of the nations which think their salvation lies in the profession of its creed? How is it that a religion avowedly making peace and long-suffering of injury the corner-stone of its temple has had as its principal outcome war, both the fanaticism of religious war and the avarice of civil war; a legislation founded on the *lex talionis* and inexorable in its adherence to that law; and a commerce with the base desire to over-reach, outwit and outstrip all competitors?"

OUIDA on ITALIAN JUSTICE:

"There is not even the gloss of affected legality in the countless arrests which have filled to overflowing the prisons of Italy. The charges by which these arrests are excused are so wide that they are a net into which all fish, big and little, may be swept. The imputation of 'inciting to hatred between the classes' is so vague that it may include almost any expression of social or political opinion. It is an accusation under which almost every great writer, thinker or philosopher would be liable to arrest, and under which Jesus Christ and Jean Jacques Rousseau, Garibaldi and John Milton, Washington and Brahma, Tolstoi and St Paul would be all alike condemned as criminals."

THE SINS OF SOCIETY

AND OTHER ESSAYS

by

OUIDA

ADELAIDE

MICHAEL WALMER

2016

These essays first published as per contents listing
Thereafter published in *View and Opinions* 1895
This collection published 2016

by

Michael Walmer
49 Second Street
Gawler South
South Australia 5118

ISBN 978-0-9944306-9-4 paperback

TO

W. H. MALLOCK

AS A SLIGHT TOKEN OF PERSONAL REGARD
AND INTELLECTUAL ADMIRATION

CONTENTS

THE SINS OF SOCIETY

'Ses divertissements sont infiniment moins raisonnables que
ses ennuis.'—PASCAL.

A BRILLIANT and daring thinker lately published some admirable papers called 'Under
the Yoke of the Butterflies.' The only thing which
I would have changed in those delightful satires
would have been the title. There are no butterflies
in this fast, furious and fussy age. They all died
with the eighteenth century, or if a few still lingered
on into this, they perished forever with the dandies.
The butterfly is a creature of the most perfect taste,
arrayed in the most harmonious colours: the butterfly is always graceful, leisurely, aerial, unerring in
its selection of fragrance and freshness, lovely as the
summer day through which it floats. The dominant
classes of the present day have nothing in the least
degree akin to the butterflies; would to Heaven that
they had! Their pleasures would be more elegant,
their example more artistic, their idleness more
picturesque than these are now. They would rest

A

peacefully on their roses instead of nailing them to
a ballroom wall; they would hover happily above
their lilies and carnations without throwing them
about in dust and dirt at carnivals.

Butterflies never congregate in swarms; it is only
locusts which do that. Butterflies linger with lan-
guorous movement, always softly rhythmical and
undulating even when most rapid, through the sunny
air above the blossoming boughs. The locust is
jammed together in a serried host, and tears breathlessly forward without knowing in the least why or
where he goes, except that he must move on and
must devour. There is considerable analogy between the locust and society; none between society
and the butterfly. But be the yoke called what it
will, it lies heavily on the world, and there is no
strength in the strongest sufficient to lift it up and
cast it off, for its iron is Custom and its ropes are
Foolishness and Bad Example, and what is termed
Civilisation carries it as the steer carries the nose-
ring and the neck-beam.

Some clever people have of late been writing a
great deal about society, taking English society as
their especial theme. But there are certain facts and
features in all modern society which they do not
touch: perhaps they are too polite, or too politic.
In the first place they seem to except, even whilst
attacking them, smart people as elegant people, and
to confuse the two together: the two words are
synonymous in their minds, but are far from being
so in reality. Many leaders of the smart sets are
wholly unrefined in taste, loud in manner, and followed merely because they please certain person-

ages, spend or seem to spend profusely, and are seen at all the conspicuous gatherings of the season in London and wherever else society congregates. This is why the smart sets have so little refining influence on society. They may be common, even vulgar; it is not necessary even for them to speak grammatically; if they give real jewels with their cotillon toys and have a perfect artist at the head of their kitchens, they can become 'smart,' and receive royalty as much and as often as they please. The horrible word smart has been invented on purpose to express this: smartness has been borrowed from the vocabulary of the kitchenmaids to express something which is at the top of the fashion, without being necessarily either well born or well bred. Smart people may be both the latter, but it is not necessary that they should be either. They may be smart by mere force of chance, impudence, charm, or the faculty of making a royal bored one laugh.

It is, therefore, impossible for the smart people to have much influence for good on the culture and manners of the society they dominate. A *beau monde*, really exclusive, elegant and of high culture, not to be bought by any amount of mere riches or display, would have a great refining influence on manner and culture, and its morality, or lack of it, would not matter much. Indeed, society cannot be an accurate judge of morality; the naughty clever people know well how to keep their pleasant sins unseen; the candid, warm-hearted people always sin the sole sin which really injures anybody—they get found out. 'You may break all the ten commandments every day if you like,' said Whyte Melville, 'provided only you observe the eleventh, "Thou shalt not be found out."' There is a morality or immorality, that of the passions, with which society ought to have little or nothing to do; but there is another kind with which it should have a good deal to do, *i.e.*, the low standard of honour and principle which allows persons in high place to take up *richards* for sheer sake of their wealth, and go to houses which have nothing to recommend them except the fact that convenient rendezvous may be arranged at them, or gambling easily prosecuted in them. But it is not society as constituted at the present year of grace which will have either the courage or the character to do this. Theoretically, it may condemn what it calls immorality and gambling, but it will always arrange its house-party in accord with the affinities which it sedulously remembers and ostensibly ignores, and will allow bac' to follow coffee after dinner rather than illustrious persons should pack up and refuse to return.

At risk of arousing the censure of readers, I confess that I would leave to society a very large liberty in the matter of its morality or immorality, if it would only justify its existence by any originality, any grace, any true light and loveliness. In the face of its foes lying grimly waiting for it, with explosives in their pockets, society should justify its own existence by its own beauty, delicacy and excellence of choice and taste. It should, as Auberon Herbert has said, be a centre whence light should radiate upon the rest of the world. But one can only give what one has, and as it has no clear light or real joy within itself it cannot diffuse them, and in all probability never will. 'The Souls' do, we know, strive in their excellent intentions and their praiseworthy faith to produce them, but they are too few in numbers, and are already too tightly caught in the tyres of the great existing machinery to be able to do much towards this end. After all, a society does but represent the temper of the age in which it exists, and the faults of the society of our time are the faults of that time itself; they are its snobbishness, its greed, its haste, its slavish adoration of a royalty which is wholly out of time and keeping with it, and of a wealth of which it asks neither the origin nor the solidity, and which it is content only to borrow and bask in as pigs in mud.

It is not luxury which is enervating; it is over-eating, over-smoking, and the poisoned atmosphere of crowded rooms. Edmond de Goncourt likes best to write in a grey, bare room which contains nothing to suggest an idea or distract the imagination. But few artists or poets would desire such an *entourage*. Beauty is always inspiration. There is nothing in a soft seat, a fragrant atmosphere, a well-regulated temperature, a delicate dinner, to banish high thought; on the contrary, the more refined and lovely the place the happier and more productive ought to be the mind. Beautiful things can be created independently of place; but the creator of them suffers when he can enjoy beauty only in his dreams. I do not think that the rich enjoy beauty one whit more than the poor in this day. They are in too great a hurry to do so. There is no artistic enjoyment without repose. Their beautiful rooms are scarcely seen by them except when filled with a throng. Their beautiful gardens and parks are visited by them rarely and reluctantly.

Their treasures of art give them no pleasure unless they believe them unique, unequalled. Their days, which might be beautiful, are crammed with incessant engagements, and choked with almost incessant eating.

In England the heavy breakfasts, the ponderous luncheons, the long, tedious dinners, not to speak of the afternoon teas and the liqueurs and spirits before bedtime, fill up more than half the waking hours; 'stoking,' as it is elegantly called, is the one joy which never palls on the human machine, until he pays for it with dyspepsia and gout. People who live habitually well should be capable of denying their appetites enough to pass from London to Paris, or Paris to London, without wanting to eat and drink. But in point of fact they never dream of such denial of the flesh, and they get out at the buffets of Boulogne and Amiens with alacrity, or order both breakfast and dinner, with wines at choice, in the club-train. A *train de luxe* is, by the the way, the epitome and portrait of modern society; it provides everything for the appetite; it gives cushions, newspapers and iced drinks; it whirls the traveller rapidly from capital to capital; but the steam is in his nostrils, the cinder dust is in his eyes, and the roar of the rattling wheels is in his ears. I do not think that plain living and high thinking are a necessary alliance. Good food, delicate and rich, is like luxury; it should not be shunned, but enjoyed. It is one of the best products of what is called civilisation, and should be duly appreciated by all those who can command it. But feeding should not occupy the exaggerated amount of time which is given to it in society, nor cost the enormous amount of money which is at present spent on it.

Luxury in itself is a most excellent thing, and I would fain see it more general, as the luxury of the bath was in Imperial Rome open to one and all ; with the water streaming over the shining silver and snowy marbles, and the beauty of porphyry and jade and agate gleaming under the silken awning, alike for plebeian and patrician. It is not for its luxury for a moment that I would rebuke the modern world : but for its ugly habits, its ugly clothes, its ugly hurry-skurry, whereby it so grossly disfigures, and through which it scarcely even perceives or enjoys the agreeable things around it.

Luxury is the product and result of all the more delicate inventions and combinations of human intelligence and handicraft. To refuse its graces and comforts would be as unwise as to use a rudely-sharpened flint instead of a good table-knife. A far more lamentable fact than the existence of luxury is that it is so little enjoyed and so rarely made general. We deliberately surrender the enjoyment of the luxury of good cooking because we most stupidly mix up eating with talking, and lose the subtle and fine flavours of our best dishes because we consider ourselves obliged to converse with somebody on our right or our left whilst we eat them. We neutralise the exquisite odours of our finest flowers by the scent of wines and smoking dishes. We spoil our masterpieces of art by putting them together pell-mell in our rooms, smothered under a discordant mingling of different objects and various styles. We allow nicotines to poison the breath of our men and women. We desire a crowd on our stairs and a crush in our rooms as evidence of our popularity and our distinction. We cannot support eight days of the country without a saturnalia of slaughter. We are so tormented by the desire to pack forty-eight hours into twenty-four, that we gobble our time up breathlessly without tasting its flavour, as a greedy schoolboy gobbles up stolen pears without peeling them. Of the true delights of conversation, leisure, thought, art and solitude, society *en masse* has hardly more idea than a flock of geese has of Greek. There is in the social atmosphere, in the social life of what is called 'the world,' a subtle and intoxicating influence which is like a mixture of champagne and opium, and has this in common with the narcotic, that it is very difficult and depressing to the taker thereof to leave it off and do without it. As La Bruyère said of the court life of his time, it does not make us happy but it makes us unable to find happiness elsewhere. After a full and feverish season we have all known the reaction which follows on the return to a quiet life. There is a magnetic attraction in the great giddy gyrations of fashionable and political life. To cede to this magnetism for a while may be highly beneficial ; but to make of it the vital necessity of existence, as men and women of the world now do, is as fatal as the incessant use of any other stimulant or opiate.

The great malady of the age is the absolute inability to support solitude, or to endure silence.

Statesmanship is obscured in babbling speech ; art and literature are represented by mere hurried impressions snatched from unwillingly - accorded moments of a detested isolation ; life is lived in a throng, in a rush, in a gallop ; the day was lost to

Titus if it did not record a good action; the day is lost to the modern man and woman unless it be spent in a mob. The horror of being alone amounts in our time to a disease. To be left without anybody else to amuse it fills the modern mind with terror. 'La solitude n'effraie pas le penseur: il y a toujours quelqu'un dans la chambre,' a witty writer has said; but it is the wit as well as the fool in this day who flies from his own company; it is the artist as well as the dandy who seeks the boulevard and the crowd.

There is nothing more costly than this hatred of one's own company, than this lack of resources and occupations independent of other persons. What ruins ninety-nine households out of a hundred is the expense of continual visiting and inviting. Everybody detests entertaining, but as they all know that they must receive to be received, and they cannot bring themselves to support solitude, people ruin themselves in entertainment. There can scarcely be a more terrible sign of decadence than the indifference with which the *grands de la terre* are everywhere selling their collections and their libraries. Instead of altering the excessive display and expenditure which impoverish them, and denying themselves that incessant amusement which they have grown to consider a necessity, they choose to sell the books, the pictures and the manuscripts which are the chief glories of their homes; often they even sell also their ancestral woods.

This day, as I write, great estates which have been in the same English family for six hundred years are going to the hammer. This ghastly necessity may be in part brought about by agricultural depression, but it is far more probably due to the way of living of the times which must exhaust all fortunes based on land. If men and women were content to dwell on their estates, without great display or frequent entertainment, their incomes would suffice in many cases. It is not the old home which ruins them : it is the London house with its incessant expenditure, the house-parties with their replica of London, the women's toilettes, the men's shooting and racing and gaming, the Nile boat, the Cairene winter, the weeks at Monte Carlo, the Scotch moors, the incessant, breathless round of intermingled sport and pleasure danced on the thin ice of debt, and kept up frequently for mere appearances' sake, without any genuine enjoyment, only from a kind of false shame and a real inability to endure life out of a crowd.

There is a stimulant and a drug, as I have said, in the curious mixture of excitement and *ennui*, of animation and fatigue, produced by society, and without this mixture the man and woman of the world cannot exist ; and to find the purchase-money of this drug is what impoverishes them, and makes them indifferent to their own degradation, and sends their beautiful old woods and old books and old pictures to the shameful uproar of the sale-rooms. If the passion for the slaughter of tame creatures which is almost an insanity, so absorbing and so dominant is it, could be done away with in England, and the old houses be really lived in by their owners all the year round with genuine affection and scholarly taste, as they were lived in by many families in Stuart and Georgian days, their influence over the counties and the villages would be incalculable and admirable, as Mr Auberon

Herbert and Mr Frederick Greenwood have recently said ; and the benefit accruing to the fortunes of the nobles and gentry would be not less.

It is not only in England that men have become bored by and neglectful of their great estates. All over Italy stand magnificent villas left to decay or tenanted by peasants, the lizard creeping in the crevices of forgotten frescoes, the wild vine climbing over the marbles of abandoned sculptures, the oranges and the medlars falling ungathered on the mosaics of the mighty and desolate courts. Why is this? In the earlier centuries men and women loved pleasure well, and had few scruples; yet they loved and honoured their country houses, and were happy in their fragrant alleys and their storied chambers, and spent magnificently on their adornment and enrichment with a noble pride. It is only now in the latest years of the nineteenth century that these superb places are left all over Europe to dust, decay, and slow but sure desolation, whilst the owners spend their time in play or speculation, call for bocks and brandies in the club-rooms of the world, and buy shares in mushroom building companies.

Marion Crawford observes dryly 'that it is useless to deny the enormous influence of brandy and games of chance on the men of the present day.' It is indeed so useless that no one who knows anything of our society would dream of attempting to deny it, and if we substitute morphia for brandy, we may say much the same of a large proportion of the women of the present day. Drinking and gambling, in some form or another, is the most general vice of the cultured world, which censures the island labourer for his beer and skittles, and condemns the continental workman for his absinthe and lotteries. It is a strange form of progress which makes educated people incapable of resisting the paltry pleasures of the green-table and the glass ; a strange form of culture which ends at the spirit frame, the playing cards, and the cigar box. The poor Japanese coolie amongst the lilies and lilacs of his little garden is surely nearer both culture and progress than the drinker and the gambler of the modern clubs.

Reflect on the enormous cost of a boy's education when he belongs to the higher strata of social life, and reflect, also, that as soon as he becomes his own master he will, in ninety-nine cases out of a hundred, take advantage of his liberty only to do what Crawford's young Don Orsino does, *i.e.*, drink brandy, gamble at bac', and try to gain admittance into the larger gaming of the Bourses. It will certainly be allowed by any dispassionate judge, that a better result might be arrived at with such exorbitant cost ; that a nobler animal ought to be produced by such elaborate and wholly useless training.

Drinking and gambling (in varied forms it is true, but in essence always the same) are the staple delights of modern life, whether in the rude western shanty of the navvy, the miner and the digger, or in the luxurious card-rooms of the clubs and the country houses of the older world. We have even turned all the rest of creation into living dice for us, and the horse trots or gallops, the dog is fastened to the show-bench, the pigeon flies from the trap, even the rat fights the terrier that our fevered pulses may beat still quicker in the unholy agitation of a gamester's greed.

We are great gamblers, and the gambler is always a strangely twisted mixture of extravagance and meanness. Expenditure is not generosity; we are lavish but we are not liberal; we will waste two thousand pounds on an entertainment, but we cannot spare five pounds for a friend in distress. For the most part we live not only up to but far beyond our incomes, and the necessary result is miserliness in small things and to those dependent on us.

' Ses divertissements sont infiniments moins raisonnables que ses ennuis,' says Pascal of the society of his day, and the statement stands good of our own. Society has no pleasure which is graceful or elevating, except music ; but music listened to in a crowd loses half its influence ; and it is an insult to the most spiritual of all the arts to regard it, as it is regarded in society, as a mere interlude betwixt dinner and the card-table. There is little except music which is beautiful in the pageantries of this day. A ball is still a pretty sight if it takes place in a great house, and if not too many people have been invited. But except this, and this only in a great house, all entertainments are unsightly. No decoration of a dinner-table, no gold plate, and orchidæ, and electric light, and old china can make even tolerable, artistically speaking, the sight of men and women sitting bolt upright close together taking their soup around it. A full concert-room, lecture-room, church, are a hideous sight. A garden party in fair weather and fine grounds alone has a certain grace and charm ; but garden parties, like all other modern spectacles, are spoilt by the attire of the men, the most frightful, grotesque and disgraceful male costume which the world has ever seen. When the archæologists of the future dig up one of our bronze statues in trousers they will have no need to go further for evidence of the ineptitude and idiotcy of the age. What our historians call the dark ages had costumes, alike for the villein and the seigneur, adapted to their needs, serviceable, picturesque and comely; this age alone, which vaunts its superiority, has a clothing for its men which is at once utterly unsightly, unhealthy, and so constructed that all the bodily beauty of an Apollo or an Achilles would be obscured, caricatured, and deformed by it. The full height of its absurdity is reached when the glazier comes in his black suit to mend your windows, and brings his working clothes in a bundle to be put on ere he works and put off ere he goes into the street. The political incapacity with which the natives of Ireland are charged by English statesmen never seemed to me so conclusively proven as by their persistence in wearing ragged tail-coats and battered tall hats in their stony fields and on their sodden bogs. A man who cannot clothe his own person reasonably is surely a man incapable of legislating for himself and for his kind. This rule, however, if acted on, would disfranchise Europe and the United States.

To a society which had any true perception of beauty, grace, or elegance, the masher would be impossible ; the shoulder-handshake, the tall hat, the eternal cigarette, the stiff collar, the dead birds on the ball-dresses and bonnets, the perspiring struggles of the sexes on the tennis ground, and a thousand other similar things would not be for a moment endured. To a society which had any high standard of refinement such entertainments as are appropriately called

' crushes' would be insupportable; the presence and
the speeches of women on public platforms would be
intolerable; all the enormities of the racecourse would
be abhorrent; its fine ladies would no more wear
dead humming-birds upon their gowns than they
would wear the entrails of dead cats; its fine gentlemen would no more gather together to murder hand-
fed pheasants than they would shoot kittens or
canaries; to a truly elegant society everything barbarous, grotesque and ungraceful would be impossible.

An incessant and *maladif* restlessness has become
the chief characteristic of all cultured society nowadays: it is accounted a calamity beyond human endurance to be six months at a time in one place; to
remain a year would be considered cause for suicide.
The dissatisfaction and feverishness which are the
diseases of the period are attributed to place most
wrongly, for change of place does not cure them and
only alleviates them temporarily and briefly. Here,
again, the royal personages are the first offenders and
the worst examples. They are never still. They
are never content. They are incessantly discovering
pretexts for conveying their royal persons here and
there, to and fro, in ceaseless, useless, costly and
foolish journeys.

Every event in their lives is a cause or an excuse
for their indulgence in the *pérégrinomanie;* if they are
well, they want change of scene; if they are ill, they
want change of air; if they suffer a bereavement,
nothing can console them except some agreeable
foreign strand; and the deaths, births and marriages
of their innumerable relations furnish them with continual and convenient reasons for incessant gyrations.

In all these multiplied and endless shiftings of place and person the photographs fly about in showers, and the gold and silver offerings are tendered in return on bended knees.

It must be confessed that royalty confirms and keeps up many usages and obligations of society which are absurd and unpleasant, and which without royal support would die a natural death.

What can be more absurd, more childish, and more utter waste of money than the salutes with which it is the custom to celebrate the going and coming, the births and the deaths, of these royal people? The savage who expresses his joy by discharging his rusty musket is deemed a silly creature ; but the civilised nation is less excusably silly which expresses its pleasure, its grief, and its homage by means of this hard, ugly, unpleasant noise which has no sense in it, and blows away in smoke vast sums of money which might easily be better spent. It is a barbarous practice, and it is difficult to comprehend a civilised world tamely submitting to its continuance.

The most vulgar form of salutation, the shake-hands, has been adopted and generalised by princes, until it is now usual in countries where it was unknown in the beginning of the century. Nothing can be more ludicrous and ungraceful, or more disagreeable, than the ' pump-handling ' which is common in all ranks of society, and which great personages might easily have abolished altogether. They think it makes them popular, and so they resort to it on every suitable and unsuitable occasion. There can be no possible reason why people should go through this unpleasant action, and few sights are more absurd than to see two elderly gentlemen solemnly sawing each other's arms up and down as they meet before the doorsteps of their club. The slight smile and scarcely perceptible bend of the head which are all with which well-bred people recognise their acquaintances at a reception or a ball, is fully sufficient for all purposes of recognition at any period of the day, and can amply preface conversation. The pressure of hands should be left to lovers, or to friends in moments of impulses of emotion ; on leave-taking before, or on welcome after, a long absence. There are many men still in Europe, not all old men either, who know how to greet a woman, and bend low over her hand and touch it lightly with their lips ; and how graceful, how respectful, how suggestive of homage is that courtly salutation ! It is the fault of women that it has become the exception, not the rule.

If we had Charles the First on the throne of England, and Louis Quatorze on the throne of France, whatever political difficulties might come of it, manners would certainly be considerably altered, corrected and refined. The influence of some great gentleman might do much to purge the coarseness and commonness of society out of it ; but such a personage does not exist, and if he did exist, the Augean stable would probably be too much for his strength. He would retire, like Beckford, to some Fonthill and build a Chinese Wall between him and the world.

But alas ! the vulgarity of the age is at its highest in high places. The position of sovereigns and their descendants is one which should at least allow them to be the first gentry of their countries in feeling as

B

they are in precedence and etiquette; they might, were they capable of it, set an example of grace, of elegance, and of purity of taste. Strong as is the revolutionary leaven amongst the masses, the force of snobbism is stronger still, and all habits and examples which come from the palace are followed by the people with eager and obsequious servility. If, when princes and princesses were united in wedlock, they ordained 'No presents,' the abominable blackmail levied by betrothed people on their acquaintances would cease to be fashionable, and would soon become 'parcel and portion of the dreadful past.' If, when princes and princesses paid the debt of nature, the Court officials sent out the decree 'No flowers,' all other classes would take example, and the horrible, senseless barbarism of piling a mass of decaying wreaths and floral crosses upon a coffin and a grave would pass to the limbo of all other extinct barbaric and grotesque customs. But they are careful to do nothing of the kind. The bridal gifts are too welcome to them; and the funeral baked meats are too savoury; and all the royal people all over Europe unite in keeping up these tributes levied from a groaning world. Modern generations have made both marriage and death more absurd, more banal, and more vulgar than any other period ever contrived to do; and it is not modern princes who will endeavour to render either of them simple, natural and dignified, for the essence and object of all royal life in modern times is vulgarity, *i.e.*, publicity.

Of all spectacles which society flocks to see, it may certainly be said that the funeral and the wedding are the most intolerably coarse and clumsy. There is indeed a curious and comical likeness between these two. Both take place in a crowd ; both are the cause for extortion and expenditure ; both are attended unwillingly and saluted with false formulæ of compliment ; both are 'seen out' and 'got through' with sighs of relief from the spectators ; and both are celebrated with the sacrifice of many myriads ·of flowers crucified in artificial shapes in their honour.

Hymen and Pallida Mors alike grin behind the costly and senseless orchids and the sweet dying roses and lilies of the jubilant nurseryman. The princes and the tradespeople have in each case decreed that this shall be so ; and society has not will or wisdom enough to resist the decree.

A poet died not long ago and left amongst his farewell injunctions the bidding to put no flowers on his bier. The wise press and public exclaimed, 'How strange that a poet should hate flowers !' Poor fools·! He loved them so deeply, so intensely, that the tears would start to his eyes when he beheld the first daffodils of the year, or leaned his lips on the cool pallor of a cluster of tea roses. It was because he loved them so well that he forbade their crucified beauty being squandered, to fade and rot upon his coffin. Every true lover of flowers would feel the same. Nothing more disgusting and more offensive can be imagined than the cardboard and wires on which the tortured blossoms are fastened in various shapes to languish in the heated atmosphere of a *chambre ardente*, or in the sickly and oppressive air of a mortuary chamber. All the designs which serve to symbolise the loves of cook and potboy on St Valentine's Day are now pressed into the service of the princely or noble mourners ; harps, crowns, crosses, hearts, lyres, and all the trash of the vulgarest sentiment are considered touching and exquisite when hung before a royal catafalque or heaped upon a triple coffin of wood, lead and velvet. In all these grotesque and vulgar shapes the innocent blossoms are nailed, gummed, or wired by workpeople, grinning and smoking as they work, and the whole mass is heaped together on bier, in crypt, or on monument, and left to rot and wither in sickening emblem of the greater corruption which it covers.

The fresh-gathered flowers laid by maidens' hands on the wet hair of Ophelia, or the white breast of Juliet, might have beauty both natural and symbolical. One spray of some best - loved blossom, placed by some best-loved hand on the silenced heart, may have the meaning and be the emblem of the deepest feeling. To put softly down upon a bed of moss and rose-leaves the dead white limbs of a little child may have fitness and beauty in the act. To go in the dusk of dawn into the wet, green ways of gardens, silent save for the call of waking birds, and gather some bud or leaf which was dear to our lost love, and bear it within to lie with him where we can never console or caress him in his eternal solitude : this may be an impulse tender and natural even in those first hours of bereavement. But to arise from our woe to order a florist to make a harp of lilies with strings of gold or silver wire ; to stay our tears, to break the seals of boxes come by rail from Nice and Grasse and Cannes : this indeed is to fall into bathos beside which the rudest funeral customs of the savage look respectable and dignified.

When we realise what death is and what it means :
that never will those lips touch ours again ; that never
will that voice again caress our ear ; that never more
will our inmost thoughts be mirrored in those eyes ;
that never more shall we say, 'Shall we do this to-
day ? shall we do that to-morrow ?' that never more
can we go together through the grass of spring, or together watch the sun drop down behind the hills ;
that never can we ask pardon if our love were
fretful, human, weak ; that never more can there be
communion or comprehension ; that all is silent, lonely,
ended, an unchanging and unchangeable desolation :
—when we realise this, I say, and think that there
are persons who, left to this awful solitude, can give
orders to floral tradesmen and take comfort in toys of
cardboard and wire, we may be pardoned if we feel
that the most bitter scorn of the cynic for human
nature is flagellation too merciful for its triviality and
folly.

Truly, in nine times out of ten it is but a conventional and unreal sorrow which thus expresses itself ;
truly, out of the millions of deaths which take place
there are but few which create deep and abiding grief ;
still, the association of these elaborate artificial wreaths
and garlands, these stiff and crucified blossoms, with
the tomb would only be possible to the most vulgar
and insensible of generations, even as decoration,
even as mere common-place compliment, whilst to the
true lover of flowers they must be ever a distressing
outrage.

In Lopez de Vega's *Diego de Alcala* the humble
servant of a poor hermit, lowliest of the low, begs
pardon of the flowers which he gathers for the chapel,

and begs them to forgive him for taking them away from their beloved meadows. This is a worthier attitude before those divine children of the dews and sun than the indifference of the lovers of the flower carnival or the funeral pageant.

If a daisy were but as scarce as a diamond, how would the multitudes rush to adore the little golden-eyed star in the grass!

One of the most exquisitely beautiful things I ever saw in my life was a thick tuft of harebell glittering all over with dew on a sunny morning where it grew on a mossy wall. It was not worth sixpence, yet it was a thing to kneel down before and adore and remember reverently for evermore.

Who will deliver us, asks George Sala, from the fashionable bridal, from the eternal ivory satin and the ghastly orange-blossom, and the two little shavers masquerading as pages?

The roughest and rudest marriage forms of savage nations are less offensive than those which are the received and admired custom of the civilised world. There cannot be a more Philistian jumble of greed, show, indecency and extravagance than are compressed into the marriage festivities of the cities of Europe and America. When the nuptials are solemnised in the country, something of country simplicity and freshness may enter into them, but almost all fashionable weddings are now taken to the cities, because a huge enough crowd cannot be gathered together even in the biggest of big country houses. Often the persons concerned go to an hotel, or borrow a friend's mansion for the celebration of the auspicious event.

Year after year the same trivial and tiresome usage,
the same vulgar and extravagant customs, the same
barbarous and uncouth ceremonies prevail, and are
accepted as sacred and unalterable law.   The most
intimate, the most delicate, the most personal actions
and emotions of life are set out in the full glare of
light in the most unscreened and most unsparing
publicity ; and no one sees the odious and disgusting
coarseness of it all.   The more sensitive and refined
temperaments submit meekly to the torture of its
commands.

If marriage, so long as the institution lasts, could
become in its celebration that which decency and
good taste would suggest, a simple and sacred rite
with neither publicity nor gaudy expenditure to profane it, there might come, with such a change, similar
alteration in other ceremonies, and sentiment might
have a chance to put in its modest plea for place un-
frightened by the loud beating of the brazen drums
of wealth.   In all the annals of the social life of the
world there has not been anything so atrocious in
vulgarity as a fashionable wedding, whether viewed in
its greedy pillaging of friends and acquaintances or in
its theatrical pomp of costume, of procession and of
banquet.   It is the very apogee of bad taste, incon-
gruity and indecency, from the coarse words of its
rites to its sputtering champagne, its unvaried orations,
and its idiotic expenditure.   It is this publicity which
is dear to the soul of our Gaius and Gaia ; for were it
not so there would be more special licences demanded,
since these are not so costly that gentle-people could
not easily afford to have their marriage ceremony as
entirely private as they pleased.   But they would not

feel any pleasure at privacy; they despise it; they
are always ready with gag and rouge for the foot-
lights ; if they had not an audience the bride and
bridegroom would yawn in each other's faces.   Every
ceremony duly repeats and carefully imitates those
which have preceded it.   There is no originality,
there is no modesty, there is no dignity or reserve.
The plunder which is called 'presents' are laid out
on exhibition, and the feverish anxiety of every bride-
elect is to get more presents than any of her contemporaries.   Even the in-door and out-door servants
of each of the two households have this shameless
blackmail levied on them ; and gillies subscribe for a
hunting-watch, and kitchen-maids contribute to the
purchase of a silver-framed mirror.   Scarcely even is
a royal or aristocratic marriage announced than the
laundries and the pantries are ransacked for sovereigns and half-sovereigns to purchase some costly
article to be offered to their princely or noble employers.   Imagine the slaves of Augustus presenting
him with a gold whistle, or the comedians of Louis
Quatorze offering him a silver cigar-box !

But all is fish which comes to the nets of the im-
pecunious great folks of the *fin de siècle*, and the
unhappy households must submit and buy a propiti-
atory gift out of their salaries.   That households are
notoriously dishonest in our day is but a necessary
consequence.   Who can blame a servant if, knowing
the blackmail which will be levied on him, he recoups
himself with commissions levied in turn upon tradesmen, or perquisites gleaned from the wine-cellars ?
It is said openly, though I cannot declare with what
truth, that all the gifts in gold and silver and jewels

which are offered to princes on their travels by loyal
corporations or adoring colonists are sold immediately,
whilst all the costly boxes and jewelled trifles which
such princes are obliged by custom to leave behind
them wherever they have been received are simi-
larly disposed of by the greater number of their
recipients. It is, perhaps, the reason why royal donors
so frequently limit themselves to the cheap gift of a
signed photograph. They know that photographs
cannot be offered to them in return.

The diffusion of German influence, which has been
general over Europe through the fatality which has
seated Germans on all the thrones of Europe, has had
more than any other thing to do with the vulgarisa-
tion of European society. The German eats in public,
kisses in public, drags all his emotions out into the
public garden or coffee-house, makes public his curious
and nauseous mixture of sugar and salt, of jam and
pickles, alike in his sentiments and in his cookery, and
praises Providence and embraces his betrothed with
equal unction under the trees of the public square.

And the influence of courts being immense, socially
and personally, society throughout Europe has been
Germanised ; scholars love to point out the far-reach-
ing and deeply penetrating influence of the Greek
and Asiatic spirit upon Rome and Latium ; historians
in a time to come will study as curiously the effect of
the German influence on the nineteenth and twentieth
centuries, and that of royal houses upon nations in an
epoch when royalty drew near its end.

It is to German and royal influence that English
society owes the introduction of what are called silver
and golden weddings, of which the tinsel sentiment

and the greedy motive are alike most unlovely.
Gaius and Gaia grown old, proclaim to all their
world that they have lived together for a quarter or a
half century in order that this fact, absolutely uninteresting to any one except themselves, may bring
them a shower of compliments and of gifts. They
may very probably have had nothing of union except
its semblance; they may have led a long life of
bickering, wrangling and dissension; Gaius may
have wished her at the devil a thousand times, and
Gaia may have opened his letters, paid his debts out
of her dower, and quarrelled with his tastes ever since
their nuptials: all this is of no matter whatever; the
twenty-five or the fifty years have gone by, and are
therefore celebrated as one long hymn of peace and
harmony, the loving-cup is passed round, and blackmail is levied on all their acquaintances. 'Old as he
is, he makes eyes at my maid because she is young
and fresh-coloured!' says Gaia in her confidante's
ear. 'The damned old hag still pulls me up if I only
look at a pretty woman!' grumbles Gaius in his club
confidences. But they smile and kiss and go before
the audience at their golden wedding and speak the
epilogue of the dreary comedy which society has
imposed on them and which they have imposed on
society. And the buffets of their dining-hall are
the richer by so many golden flagons and caskets
and salvers given by their admiring acquaintances,
who are not their dupes but who pretend to be so in
that unending make-believe which accompanies us
from the nursery to the grave. The union may have
been virtually a separation for five-sixths of its term;
the ill temper of the man or the carping spirit of the

woman, or any one of the other innumerable causes of dissension which make dislike so much easier and more general than affection, may have made of this ' married life' an everlasting apple of discord blistering the lips which have been fastened to it. Nevertheless, because they have not been publicly separated, the wedded couple, secretly straining at their chains, are bound after a certain term of years to receive the felicitations and the gifts of those around them.

The grotesqueness of these celebrations does not seem to strike any one. This century has but little humour. In a witty age these elderly wedded pairs would be seen to be so comical, that laughter would blow out their long-lit hymeneal torch, and forbid the middle-aged or aged lovers to undraw the curtains of their nuptial couches. Love may wither in the flesh, yet keep his heart alive maybe—yes, truly—but if Love be wise, he will say nothing about his heart when his lips are faded.

Old men and women, with grandchildren by the hundred, and offspring of fifty years old, should have perception enough of the ridiculous not to speak of a union which has so many living witnesses to its fruitfulness. The tenderness which may still unite two aged people who have climbed the hill of life together, and are together descending its slope in the grey of the coming night, may be one of the holiest, as it is certainly the rarest, of human sentiments, but it is not one which can bear being dragged out into the glare of publicity. What is respectable, and even sacred, murmured between ' John Anderson my jo, John,' and his old wife as they sit in the evening on the moss-grown wall of the churchyard, where they will soon be laid side by side together for evermore, is ridiculous and indecent when made the theme of after-dinner speeches and newspaper paragraphs. No true feeling should ever be trumpeted abroad ; and the older men and women grow, the more bounden on them becomes the reserve which can alone preserve their dignity. But dignity is the quality in which the present period is most conspicuously deficient. Those who possess it in public life are unpopular with the public ; those who possess it in private life are thought pretentious, or old-fashioned and stiff-necked.

The French expression for being fashionable, *dans le train*, exactly expresses what fashion now is. It is to be remarkable in a crowd indeed, but still always in a crowd, rushing rapidly with that crowd, and no longer attempting to lead, much less to stem it. Life lived at a gallop may be, whilst we are in the first flight, great fun, but it is wholly impossible that it should be very dignified. The cotillon cannot be the minuet. The cotillon is sometimes a very pretty thing, and sometimes a very diverting one, but it is always a romp. I would keep the cotillon, but I would not force every one to join in it. Society does force every one to do so, metaphorically speaking ; you must either live out of the world altogether or you must take the world's amusements as you find them, and they are nowadays terribly monotonous, and not seldom very unintelligent, and a severe drain upon both wealth and health. Youth, riches and beauty may have 'a good time,' because they contain in themselves many elements of pleasure ; but this 'good time' is at its best not elegant and always feverish ; it invents nothing, it satisfies no ideal, it is full of slavish

imitation and repetition, and it is bored by tedious
and stupid ceremonies which everyone execrates, but
no one has the courage to abolish or refuse to
attend.

One is apt to believe that anarchy will sooner or
later break up our social life into chaos because it
becomes so appalling to think that all these silly and
ugly forms of display and pompous frivolity will go
on for ever ; that humanity will be for ever snobbishly
prostrate before princes, babyishly pleased with stars
and crosses, grinningly joyful to be packed together
on a grand staircase, and idiotically impotent to
choose or to act with independence.   There appears
no possibility whatever of society redressing, purify-
ing, elevating itself; the unsavoury crowd at the
White House reception and the Elysées ball is only
still more hopelessly ridiculous and odious than the
better-dressed and better-mannered throng at St
James's or the Hofburg.   The office-holder in a republic has as many toadies and parasites as an arch-
duke or a *kronprinz*.   The man who lives in a shanty
built of empty meat and biscuit tins on the plains of
Nevada or New South Wales is by many degrees a
more degraded form of humanity than his brother
who has stayed amongst English wheat or Tuscan
olives or French vines or German pine-trees : many
degrees more degraded, because infinitely coarser and
more brutal, and more hopelessly soaked in a sordid
and hideous manner of life.   All the vices, mean-
nesses and ignominies of the Old World reproduce
themselves in the so-called New World, and become
more vulgar, more ignoble, more despicable than in
their original hemisphere.   Under the Southern Cross

of the Australian skies, cant, snobbism, corruption, venality, fraud, the worship of wealth *per se*, are more rampant, more naked, and more vulgarly bedizened than beneath the stars of Ursa Major. It is not from the mixture of Methodism, drunkenness, revolver-shooting, wire-pulling, and the frantic expenditure of *richards* who were navvies or miners a week ago, that any superior light and leading, any alteration for the better in social life can be ever looked for. All that America and Australia will ever do will be to servilely reproduce the follies and hope-lessly vulgarise the habits of the older civilisation of Europe.

What is decreasing, fading, disappearing more and more every year is something more precious than any mere enjoyment or embellishment. It is what we call high breeding ; it is what we mean when we say that *bon sang ne peut mentir.* All the unpurchasable, unteachable, indescribable qualities and instincts which we imply when we say he or she has 'race' in him, are growing more and more rare through the continual alliance of old families with new wealth. We understand the necessity of keeping the blood of our racing and coursing animals pure, but we let their human owners sully their stock with indifference so long as they can 'marry money,' no matter how that money has been made. The effect is very visible ; as visible as the deterioration in the manners of the House of Commons since neither culture nor courtesy are any longer exacted there, and as the injury done to the House of Lords by allowing it to become a retreat for retired and prosperous tradesmen.

It is reported that Ravachol, who was not especially sound at the core himself, stated it as his opinion
that society is so rotten that nothing can be done
with it except to destroy it.   Most sober thinkers,
who have not Ravachol's relish for the pastimes of
crime, must yet be tempted to agree with him.   Who
that knows anything at all of the inner working of
administrative life can respect any extant form of
government?   Who that has studied the practical
working of elective modes of choice can fail to see
that there is no true choice in their issues at all, only
endless wire-pulling?   Who can deny that all the
legislation in the world must for ever be powerless to
limit the *sub rosa* influence of the unscrupulous man?
Who can deny that in the struggle for success,
honesty and independence and candour are dead-
weights, suppleness and falsehood, and the sly tact
which bends the knee and oils the tongue, are the
surest qualities in any competitor?   Who can frame
any social system in which the enormous, intangible
and most unjust preponderance of interest and influence can be neutralised, or the still more unjust preponderance of mere numbers be counteracted?

Some thinkers predict that the coming ruler, the
working man, will change this rottenness to health;
but it may safely be predicted that he will do nothing
of the kind.   He will be at the least as selfish, as
bribable, and as vain, as the gentry who have preceded
him; he will be certainly coarser and clumsier in his
tastes, habits, and pleasures, and the narrowness of his
intelligence will not restrain the extravagance of his
expenditure of moneys not his own, with which he
will be able to endow himself by legislation.   If

Socialism would, in reality, break up the deadly monotony of modern society, who would not welcome it? But it would do nothing of the kind. It would only substitute a deadlier, a still triter monotony; whilst it would deprive us of the amount of picturesqueness, stimulant, diversity and expectation which are now derived from the inequalities and potentialities of fortune. The sole things which now save us, from absolute inanity are the various possibilities of the unexpected and the unforeseen with which the diversity of position and the see-saw of wealth now supply us. The whole tendency of Socialism, from its first tentatives in the present trades unions, is to iron down humanity into one dreary level, tedious and featureless as the desert. It is not to its doctrines that we can look for any increase of wit, of grace and of charm. Its triumph would be the reign of universal ugliness, sameness and commonness. Mr Keir Hardie in baggy yellow trousers, smoking a black pipe close to the tea-table of the Speaker's daughters, on the terrace of the House of Commons, is an exact sample of the 'graces and gladness' which the democratic' apotheosis would bestow on us.

It is not the cap and jacket of the Labour member, or the roar of the two-legged wild beasts escorting him, which will open out an era of more elegant pleasure, of more refined amusement, or give us a world more gracious, picturesque and fair. Mob rule is rising everywhere in a muddy ocean which will outspread into a muddy plain wherein all loveliness and eminence will be alike submerged. But it is not yet wholly upon us. There is still time for society, if it care to do so, to justify its own existence ere its despoilers be upon it ; and it can only be so justified if it become something which money cannot purchase, and envy, though it may destroy, cannot deride.

CONSCRIPTION

I N a recent interview with Lord Wolseley, the visitor states that he obtained from that officer the following vehement declaration in favour of enforced and universal military service :—

'You develop his physical power, you make a man of him in body and in strength, as the schools he had been at previously had made a man of him mentally. You teach him habits of cleanliness, tidiness, punctuality, reverence for superiors, and obedience to those above him, and you do this in a way that no species of machinery that I have ever been acquainted with could possibly fulfil. In fact, you give him all the qualities calculated to make him a thoroughly useful and loyal citizen when he leaves the colours and returns home to civil life. And of this I am quite certain, that the nation which has the courage and the patriotism to insist on all its sons undergoing this species of education and training for at least two or three generations, will consist of men and women far better calculated to be the fathers and mothers of healthy and vigorous children than the nation which allows its young people to grow up without any physical training although they may cram their heads with all sorts of scientific knowledge in their national schools. In other words, the race in two or three generations will be stronger, more vigorous, and therefore braver, and more calculated to make the nation to which they belong great and powerful.'

It is obvious that such a rhapsody could only be uttered by one who has never studied the actual effects of conscription on a population, but speaks merely of what he has been led to believe is its effect from what he has watched on the drill-grounds of countries little otherwise known to him. It is a sweeping assertion, still less grounded on fact than its corresponding declaration, that school makes a man of its pupil mentally, which is by no means always or inevitably the case. I could not, of course, propose to contravene any purely military statement of a military celebrity, but this composite and wholesale and most amazing declaration I do dispute, and I think that I know more of the effects of compulsory service than does its speaker. Lord Wolseley has never certainly dwelt, even for a short time, in those countries which are cursed by conscription. He sees that the battalions of conscripted armies seem to him to march well and manœuvre finely, and he concludes, with natural military prejudice, that the results, moral and mental, of conscription on a nation are admirable, and are unattainable in any other manner.

To begin with, he considers evidently as beyond all dispute that the soldier is the highest type of humanity, which may be doubted, and that obedience is the highest human virtue, which may be also doubted. All the finest freedoms of mankind have been obtained, not by obedient, but by utterly disobedient, persons ; persons who, if they had failed, would have been thrown into prison or sent to scaffolds. Obedience in the child is the first and the highest virtue, because the whole well-being of the child, material and moral, depends on it. But the man, to be a man, must be courageous enough to disobey if disobedience be needed by honour, justice, or wisdom. There are moments, even in war and even in a soldier's life, when the magnificent daring which disobeys is a more precious quality than the primmer and more decorous one of unquestioning deference to commands received. In older times the modes of warfare or the manner of civil life left much freer scope to idiosyncrasy and choice, much wider space for the play of spirit and originality. Modern warfare, like modern education, tends yearly to draw tighter the bonds with which it buckles down all natural growth of character and possibility of adventure. Mechanical reproduction is the chief note of military effort as of civil. The soldier, like the civilian, every year tends more and more to become only one infinitesimal atom of a rivet in the enormous and overwhelming engine of the State.

To a young man of genius, or even of merely great talent, it is certain that the enforced term of military service would be sorely and indelibly injurious. Genius does not easily obey, and all the harsh, unlovely, stupid routine of camp and barrack would be so odious to it that a youth of brilliant gifts and promise might easily be compromised and condemned, continually and fatally, in his passage through the ranks. Even were such a youth obedient to his duties, the sheer waste of time, the dispiriting influences of a long period of tedious, irksome, and detested occupations, would have the most depressing and dwarfing effect upon his talent. History teems with instances, which it would be tiresome to enumerate, in which revolt and refusal have produced for the world all that we most prize of liberty, of conscience, and of conduct. Revolt and refusal are disobedience, and they have frequently been quite as noble and fruitful as the more passive virtue of obedience, which not seldom has taken the form of timorous submission to, and execution of, conscious wrong. Would Lord Wolseley have admired or condemned a *mousquetaire* of the Louvre who should have refused to fire on the Huguenots from the windows?

But were obedience the first of virtues, conscription does not teach it: it enforces it, which is a very different thing. You do not put a quality into a man because you taught him and forced from him by fear the simulacrum of it. Because the conscript has for a term of years, to his bitter hatred and despite, been compelled to obey at the point of the bayonet, he does not thereby become a more willingly obedient man; he will, on the contrary, as soon as he is set free, revenge himself by insubordination to his parents, his employers, his superiors, in all the ways which may be open to him. The obedience exacted from the soldier is taken by force: he obeys because he knows that those stronger than himself will punish him badly if he do not. This is not an ennobling sentiment, nor is it one which can lend any beauty or nobility to a character. You are not a better or a kinder master because you have been a slave, nilly-willy, for three of the best years of your life. Obedience which is rendered out of true vener-ation may be a tonic to the nature which is bent by it; but the obedience which is merely rendered, as all conscripts' obedience is, because if it be not given the irons and the cell will follow, does no one any moral good, teaches no virtue which can be productive hereafter. There is no servant, groom, artisan, farm-labourer, or hireling of any kind so lazy, so impudent, so insubordinate, and so useless as the young man who has recently come out from his term of compulsory service. It is natural that it should be so. As we cannot create morality by Act of Parliament, so we cannot create character by the knapsack and the cross-belts. Family education, even school education, can in a measure mould character, because it is the long, free, malleable, tender years of childhood and boyhood upon which it works; but after twenty-one, the character does not vitally alter much, though it will assimilate vice and vanity with fatal quickness. When Lord Wolseley utters the preposterous declaration that the education given by conscription teaches a lad ' all the qualities calculated to make him a thoroughly . useful and loyal citizen,' has he the least idea of what is the actual moral state of the barrack-yards and barrack-rooms of the armies of the continent? Has he ever reflected on the inevitable results of the pell-mell confusion with which the clean-living young sons of gentle-people and commercial people are flung together with the lowest ruffians from the cellars of the cities and the caves of the mountains? Will he even credit how constantly the healthy, hard-working, obedient lad from the farmside or the counting-house, who left his people, happy in his duties and clean in body and mind, comes back to them, when his time is over, cankered body and soul, eaten up by disease, scornful of simple ways, too useless to work, too depraved to wed, too puffed up with foul desires and braggart conceits to earn the bread which he considers his father and brothers bound to labour to provide for him?

When the youth has had purity and strength of character and of mind enough to resist the contagion in which he has been steeped, he will in nine instances out of ten be a spoilt agriculturist, artisan, student, labourer. He has been torn from his chosen pursuit at the moment when he had begun to fairly master it, and he is spoilt for it, he is out of joint with it, he forgets its cunning. If he were engaged in any of those arts which require the utmost delicacy of touch, the ends of his fingers have become coarse, rough, blunted, and have lost all their sensitiveness; the porcelain - painters, the jewellers' artificers, the makers of the inimitable *articles de Paris*, suffer immeasurably from the injury done to their finger-tips by barrack work; whilst on the other hand the horny palms of the lads who push the plough and use the spade have grown so softened by what is to them the lighter work of the barracks, that they writhe with pain when they go out on their farms and the skin soon is stripped off the raw flesh.

To a military commander it is natural that the diffusion of the military temper should appear the beau ideal of improvement. Every class has its own intrinsic vanity, and sees in itself the salt and savour of society. But in truth there is a distinct menace to the world, in the present generalisation of the military temper, which is and must always be accompanied by narrowness and domination. What the young man acquires from his years of enforced service is much more often the hectoring and bullying temper characteristic of the soldier to the civilian, than it is the obedience, humility and loyalty which Lord Wolseley believes that he brings away with him. It is certainly most unjust that the soldier should be regarded, as in England, inferior to the civilian, and hustled out of theatres and concert-rooms ; but it is still worse for the community when the soldier can fire on citizens, slash at greybeards, and run through children with impunity, as he can do in Germany, at his will and pleasure.

The very rules and qualities which are inevitable for the well-being of the soldier are injurious to the character of the civilian : mill-like routine, and unquestioning acceptance of orders, are not the makers of virile or high-minded men in civil life, however necessary they may be in battalions. Linesmen and gunners are admirable and useful persons, but they are not the supreme salt of the earth that we should endeavour to make all humanity in their likeness. The military education creates a certain sort of man, an excellent sort of man in his way, and for his purpose ; but not the man who is the best product of the human race.

The story of Tell may be a myth or a fact, but whichever it be, the refusal to bow to the cap on the pole represents a heroism and a temper finer than any which militarism can teach, and which are, indeed, altogether opposed to it. Even were the regiment the school which Lord Wolseley is pleased to believe it, why should he suppose that there are no others as good or better ? The old apprenticeships, which have been done away with, were strict in discipline and insistent on obedience, and they are now considered too severe in consequence. Yet they were schools which kept a youth constantly within the practice of his art or trade. Conscription takes him away from it. It unsettles a young man at the precise moment in his life when it is most necessary that he should be confirmed in his tastes for and practice of his chosen occupation. It sends him from his village to some city, perchance hundreds of miles away, and keeps shifting him from place to place, imbuing him with the sickly fever of unrest, which is the malady of the age, and rendering his old, quiet, home-rooted life impossible to him. There can be nothing worse for him than the barrack life ; at times very harsh and onerous and cruel, but with long, lazy pauses in it of absolute idleness, when the lad, lying in the sun on the stone benches, dozes and boozes his hours away, and the vicious rogue can poison at will the ear of the simple fool.

Lord Wolseley considers it an admirable machinery for creating citizens ; it is not so, because the individual it creates is a mere machine, with no will of his own, with all virility and spirit beaten and cursed out of him, with no ideal set before him but to wait on the will of his corporal or captain. A soldier is at no time a good 'all round' man ; the military temper and standard are, and must be, always narrow. In its most odious and offensive forms, as in Germany, it amounts to a brutal and most dangerous tyranny, overbearing in its intolerable vanity, and holding civilian life of no more account than dust.

Lord Wolseley seems to imagine that where conscription exists every man serves. In no country does every man serve. Even in Germany a very large proportion escape through physique or through circumstances, through voluntary mutilation or emigration. It is fortunate that it is so, for I can conceive nothing so appalling to the world as would be the forcing of the military temper down the throats of its entire multitudes. Militarism is the negation of individuality, of originality, and of true liberty. Its sombre shadow is spread over Europe ; its garotting collar of steel is on the throat of the people. 'Forty-eight has produced nothing better than the universal rule of the tax-gatherer and the gendarme. The French Republic has the same corruption, the same tyrannies, and the same coercion by bayonets for which the two Empires were reviled. Germany is a hell of despotism, prosecution and espionage. Russia, a purely military nation, is given up to torture, corruption, filth, and drunkenness. Italy has recovered political freedom only to fall prostrate at the feet of her old foe, who has 'the double beak to more devour.' This is all that militarism and its offspring, conscription, has done for the three nations who most loudly protested their free principles. In the latter, at least, the whole people sweat, groan, perish under the burdens laid upon them for the maintenance of the vast battalions of young men imprisoned in barrack-yards in enforced idleness and semi-starvation, whilst the fruitful lands of the Veneto, of Apulia, of the Emilia, of Sardinia, and of Calabria lie untilled under the blue skies, the soil crying for its sons, the spade and the scythe rusting whilst the accursed sabre and musket shine.

When the gain of what is termed a whole nation under arms is estimated, the exaggeration of the pompous phrase hides the nakedness of the fact that large numbers of young men are lost to their country by the means to which they resort to escape military service. In Italy and Germany these may be counted by legions : in France fugitives from the military law are less numerous, because in France men are more wedded to the native soil, and take to service more gaily and more naturally, but in Italy and Germany thousands flock to emigrant ships, thus choosing life-long self-expatriation ; and every year, as the military and fiscal burdens grow heavier, will lads go away by preference to lands where, however hard be the work, the dreaded voice of the drill-sergeant cannot reach them, and they can 'call their soul their own.' Patriotism is a fine quality, no doubt, but it does not accord with the chill and supercilious apathy which characterises the general teaching and temper of this age, and a young man may be pardoned if he deem that his country is less a mother worthy of love than a cruel and unworthy stepmother, when she demands three of the fairest years of his life to be spent in a barrack-yard, and wrings his ears till the blood drops from them, or beats him about the head with the butt of a musket, because he does not hold his chin high enough, or shift his feet quickly enough.

For a hundred years humanity in this generation has been shouting, screaming, fighting, weeping, chaunting, bleeding in search and struggle for various forms of what has been called liberty. The only result hitherto deducible from this is the present fact that the nations of Europe are all watching each other like a number of sullen and suspicious dogs. We are told that this is peace. It is such excellent and perfect peace that it is merely their mutual uncertainty of each other's strength which keeps them from flying at each other's throats. It is not peace which Europe enjoys; it is an armed truce, with all the exhausting strain on the body politic and on the exchequer which must accompany such a state of things. Conscription enables this state of tension to exist, and the impatience which conscription excites in the people renders them perpetually thirsty and feverish for war. They fancy that war would end it; would give them some good in return for all their sufferings. 'We cannot go on like this,' is the universal feeling on the Continent; it is the feeling created by conscription. Conscription is the pole-axe with which the patient labourer or citizen is brained, and it is cut from the wood of his own roof-tree. It is possible, probable, that conscription will be enforced in England also, with the many other forms of servitude which democracy assures us is liberty; but it is certain that when it is so, the country will be no longer the England which we have known in history.

GARDENS

IN the charming essay called 'Caxtoniana' there
is a passage on gardens which is supremely true,
and which reminds us that whoever has a garden has
one chamber roofed by heaven in which the poet and
philosopher can feel at home. This passage was
written beside a bay-window opening on the stately
and beautiful gardens of the great author's home: to
few is it given to possess such; but of any garden a
certain little kingdom may be made, be it only green
enough and well removed from city noise. Even
within cities, little gardens, such as may be seen in
the Faubourg St Martin and the Marais, where the
population is poorest and densest, may be charm-
ingly pretty, and a great solace to those who care for
and look on them; and it is these little nooks and
corners of gardens which give so much of its joyous and glad aspect to the whole of Paris. The
great beauty of Rome (now since the Italian occupation irrevocably destroyed) was in the gardens; the
shadowy, noble, antique gardens, with the embalmed
breath of the past on their air, and the eternal youth

45

of their flowers running wild over funeral sepulchre and fortress wall. It is their gardens which make the ancient cities and towns of Belgium so full of repose, of friendliness, of the calm of Nature and the romance of history. Public gardens, like public parks, may be beautiful, useful, health-giving, pleasure-giving; but still they must ever be public gardens: it is the private gardens, the green places dedicated to thought and to affection, which alone are lovable, and which alone make a home possible, even amidst the network of crowded streets.

It would be difficult for a Thoreau or a Wordsworth, for Alfred Austin or for Alphonse Karr, to find much pleasure in a public garden even historic as that of the Luxembourg, wondrous as those of the East, or beautiful as that of the Borghese in Rome or the English garden of Munich. Wherever intrusion is possible, and any movement other than that of birds is heard, we have no garden in the fullest, sweetest sense of the word. The lover of his garden is inevitably and essentially exclusive. He must be so, or the magic charm of his domain is gone. It may be a tiny plot fenced round by a privet or box hedge, or it may be stately pleasaunces walled in by clipped yew and gay terraces; but it must be his alone; his to wander in, to cherish, to dream through, undisturbed. A public garden is a valuable pleasure-ground for a city; but is no more a garden 'roofed by heaven,' in Bulwer-Lytton's sense of the word, than life in a hotel and at a *table d'hôte* is a home.

Gardens tend sadly to become more and more artificial with the ever-increasing artificiality of an age which, whilst demanding nature from its art and literature, becomes itself, with every breath it draws, farther and farther removed from nature. The great gardens of great houses in England, esteemed the finest gardens in the world, are spoiled for those who love them by the innumerable gardeners, by the endless and overdone sweeping and cleaning and clipping and pruning. A garden, like a woman may be too neat, too stiff, too *tiré à quatre éping les*. The remorseless brooms and barrows in autumn trundle away all the lovely carpet of golden and crimson leaves, and deprive the nightingales, when they come in spring, of their favourite and most necessary retreat. Sweep the paths, if you will, though even they need not be swept as smooth as a billiard-table ; but to sweep and clear away the leaves from under the shrubberies, and from about the roots of trees, is a fatal error, most destructive to the trees themselves.

'Corisande's garden,' in 'Lothair,' is the ideal garden ; and it is pathetic to think ·that, as an ideal, it was given to the world by one esteemed of all men the coldest and most world-hardened. But Disraeli had a warm and enduring devotion to flowers in his nature, and their loveliness and innocence and 'breath of heaven' never failed to touch the soul which slumbered behind that glittering, artificial, and merciless intelligence. He rightly abhorred the elaborately-patterned beds, the dazzling assorted colours, the formal mosaic of hues, in which the modern gardener delights. All the sweet-smelling, and what are now called old-fashioned, flowers are hustled out of the way by the bedding-out system and the present craze for geometrical arrangement. Numbers of delicious flowers which were dear to the heart of Herrick, fragrant, homely, kindly, hardy things, have been banished almost out of all knowledge, that the pelargonium, the dahlia, the calceolaria, the coleus, and various other scentless but fashionable flowers may fill group and border. It is a mistake. Even the petunia and the dwarf datura, though so sweet at sunset, cannot give such fragrance as will yield the humble favourites of yore—the musk-plants, the clove-pinks, the lavender, the lemon-thyme, the moss-rose, the mignonette, and many another sweet and simple plant which is rarely now seen out of cottage gardens.

Educated taste will spend large sums of money on odontozlossom, catleyia and orchid, whilst it will not glance perhaps once in a lifetime at the ruby spots on the cowslip bells and the lovely lilac or laburnum flowers blowing in a wild west wind. It will be a sorry day for the flowers and the nation when the cottage gardens of England disappear and leave the frightful villa garden and the painfully mathematical allotment field alone in their stead. An English cottage, such as Creswick and Constable, as old Crome and David Cox saw and knew them, and as they may still be seen, with roses clambering to the eaves, and bees humming in the southern-wood and sweetbriar, and red and white carnations growing beside the balsam and the dragon's-mouth, is a delicious rural study still linked, in memory, with foaming syllabub and ruddy cherries, and honey-comb yellow as amber, and with the plaintive bleating of new-born lambs sounding beyond the garden coppice. Who that knows England has not some such picture—nay, a hundred such pictures —in his recollection?

And it is in these gardens that Shakespeare's, Milton's, Ben Jonson's 'posies' may still be gathered ; every flower and floweret of them still known by such names as Ophelia and Perdita gave them. Even in winter they are not wholly dreary or colourless ; for there are their holly-bushes, their hellebore, their rosethorn, their hepatica, and their snowdrops to enliven them. In these times, when all the 'realism' of the lives of the poor is considered to lie in squalor, famine, crime, drunkenness, and envy, it is pleasant to know that such cottage gardens as these are still extant, though no longer frequent, in the land of Shakespeare and Ben Jonson ; and that often, behind the door where the climbing white rose mounts to meet the thatch, there are still good humour, thrift, cheerfulness and cleanliness to be found in company with that manly content in existing circumstances which is the only form of durable happiness or solid virtue.

Children should never be allowed to pluck flowers, even in the fields and hedges, merely to throw them aside ; they should be early taught reverence for this floral beauty which is around them, and never be permitted wantonly to break down boughs and branches, or fill their laps with buttercups and daisies only to leave them withered in the sun, discarded and forgotten. To teach the small child to care for flowers, to place them tenderly in water when gathered, and cherish them carefully in his nursery, is not only to give him a valuable moral lesson, but to lead him also to a taste and feeling which will give him, when he grows to manhood, many glad and innocent hours, and render him thoughtful and

sympathetic when he deals with those sensitive plants,
—the souls of women.

A love for flowers indicates the quickness for imagination and the delicacy of sentiment of those in
whom it is strong. It will also be almost always
accompanied by a feeling for all other kinds of
natural beauty and woodland life. It would be
difficult to love the rose without loving the nightingale, or cherish the hawthorn without caring for
the thrushes that build in it. The fatal tendency of
modern life is to replace natural by artificial beauty,
where beauty is not driven out of the way altogether.
Every child who is led to feel the loveliness of the
water-lily lying on the green pond-water, or of the
wild hyacinth growing in the home-wood grasses, will,
as he grows up, lend his influence and his example
to the preservation of all rural and sylvan loveliness.

In the great world, and in the rich world, flowers
are wasted with painful prodigality. The thousands
and tens of thousands of flowers which die to
decorate a single ball or reception are a sad sight
to those who love them. ' The rooms look well to-
night,' is the utmost that is ever said after all this
waste of blossom and fragrance. It is waste, because
scarcely a glance is bestowed on them, and the
myriad of roses which cover the walls do not effect-
ively make more impression on the eye than the
original silk or satin wall-hanging which they
momentarily replace. Growing plants may be used
in thousands for decoration without waste, but the
inordinate display of cut flowers is a pitiable destruction of which scarcely one guest in fifty is
sensible. In bowls and baskets and jars, cut flowers

can live out their natural space; but nailed on walls, or impaled on wires, they are soon faded and yellow, and the ballroom in the morning is as melancholy a parable of the brevity of pleasure as any moralist could desire.

Church decoration is not a whit better; flowers are wantonly sacrificed to it, and in the winter the birds are starved through it for need of the evergreen berries torn down in woods and gardens to adorn the altars of men. The numbers of dead birds found in frost and snow on moor and field have increased enormously with the increase in church decoration. A sheaf of grain hung up for the seed-eating birds in winter, with some trays of meal-worms put on the ground for the insectivorous birds, would be a more useful form of piety than the cartload of branches and the garlands of berries given to church and cathedral.

The young should be led to cherish their flowers as wisely as, and more tenderly than, they cherish their gold and silver pieces in their money-boxes. The exquisite beauty of even the humblest blossom can only be appreciated by the eyes which gaze on it with attention and affection. If the wild thyme, or the shepherd's-purse, or the cuckoo's-eye, or any one of the tiny blossoms of the sward and the hedge-row were but as rare as sapphires are, the whole world would quarrel for them; but Nature has sown these little treasures broadcast with lavish hand, and scarcely any one is grateful. A single flower, if taken care of in winter, will gladden the eyes of an invalid or cripple for days; with care and thought for it a bunch of cut flowers, if cut at sunrise with the dew upon them, will live the week out in water in any cool weather ; but these lovely, joy-giving things are wasted with the most reckless indifference.

Botany may be well in its way ; but incomparably better is the practical knowledge of how to make flowers grow, and infinitely better still is the tenderness which turns aside not to tread on the wild flower in the path, not to needlessly disturb the finch's nest in the blossoming broom. Of all emotions which give the nature capable of it the purest and longest-lived pleasure, the sense of the beauty of natural things is the one which costs least pain in its indulgence, and most refines and elevates the character. The garden, the meadow, the wood, the orchard, are the schools in which this appreciative faculty is cultured most easily and enjoyably. Dostoïevsky may find food for it on the desolate steppe, and Burns in the dreary ploughed furrow ; but to do this, genius must exist in the man who feels : it is to the ordinary sensibilities, the medium mind, the character which is malleable, but in no way unusual, that this training of the eye and of the heart is necessary : and for this training there is no school so happy and so useful as a garden.

All children, or nearly all, take instinctive delight in gardens : it is very easy to make this delight not merely an instinctive, but an intelligent one; very easy to make the arrival of the first crocus, the observation of the wren's nest in the ivy hedge, of the perennial wonders of frost and of sunshine, of the death and the resurrection of Nature, of the deepest interest to a young mind athirst for marvels. Then what greater joy and triumph does the world hold than these of the child gardener with his first bouquet

of roses, his first basket of water-cress, his first hand-
ful of sweet peas! His garden, if he be taught to
care for it in the right way, will be an unceasing
happiness to him; he will not grudge the birds a
share of his cherries, for he will value too well the
songs they sing to him; he will breathe in the fresh
home balm of the dewy sweet herbs, the wet flower
borders, and he will draw in health and vigour with
every breath; and if he reads his fairy stories and his
lays of chivalry under the blossoming limes, poetry
and history will keep for him in all after time something of his first garden's grace, something of the
charm of a summer playtime.

If we did not know it as a fact, we should infer
from the whole tenor of the verse of Tennyson that
green old gardens, deep in their shade and placid in
their beauty, had been about him all his life from
infancy. The garden is a little pleasaunce of the
soul, by whose wicket the world can be shut out from
us. In the garden something of the Golden Age
still lingers; in the warm alleys where the bees hum
above the lilies and the stocks, in the blue shadows
where the azure butterflies look dark, in the amber
haze where the lime leaves and the acacia flowers
wave joyously as the west wind passes.

The true lover of a garden counts time and seasons
by his flowers. His calendar is the shepherd's
calendar. He will remember all the events of his
years by the trees or plants which were in blossom
when they happened. 'The acacias were in flower
when we first met,' or 'the hawthorns were in blossom
when we last parted,' he will say to himself, if not to
others; and no lovers are happier, or more spiritually

in love than those whose sweetest words have been spoken in a garden, and who have fancy and feeling enough to associate their mute companions in memory with their remembered joys. No love can altogether die which comes back upon remembrance with every golden tuft of daffodil or every garland of growing honeysuckle. It is the garden scene in 'Faust,' it is the garden scene in 'Romeo and Juliet,' which embody passion in its fullest and its fairest hours.

O BEATI INSIPIENTES!

'BLESSED are the poor in spirit,' says the Evangelist: he should have added, Blessed are the fools, the commonplace, the obscure, the mediocre; blessed those who have done nothing remarkable, thought nothing noteworthy, created nothing beautiful, and given nothing fair and fine to their generation! Unmolested may they dwell; unharassed may they live their lives at their own pleasure, unwatched may they take their daily walks abroad, ungrudged may they find happiness, unmolested may they indulge their grief. Their nursery days may rest forgotten; they will not be ransacked for reminiscences of childish petulance or babyish frowardness. Their school years may rest in the past, undisturbed by the grubbing of chroniclers and commentators, amongst the playground dust, and between the pages of the gradus. Their faults and follies will lie quiet in the grave, and no contemporary schoolfellow will recall their thefts of apples or their slips in parsings; or will write to the newspapers how they used a crib or smashed a

tradesman's windows.   Unworried, unenvied, unmis-
represented, they will pass through life inglorious, but
at peace ; and amongst the ashes of their buried years
no curious hands will poke and rake in feverish zeal
to find traces in their infancy of their bad passions,
and drag out the broken pieces of the rattles or the
ninepins they destroyed.

How ignorant is genius of what it does when it
leaps up to the light of its sunrise ! how little it recks
of the hornet swarm which will circle round its head, of
the viper brood which will coil round its ankles, of the
horde of stinging, prying, buzzing, poisoning insects
which will thicken the air as it passes, and hide in the
heart of the roses it gathers !

It is not only the fierce light which beats upon a
throne which genius has to bear, but the lurid glare of
the sulphur fires of envy, making livid what is white,
making hideous what is fair, making distorted and
deformed what is straight and smooth and comely.

The world holds a concave mirror to the face of
genius, and judges the face by the reflection.

The calm consciousness of power in the great writer,
in the great artist, will always appear vanity to the
majority, because the majority is incapable of seeing
how entirely different to vanity it is, and how, if
arrogant in the world, it is always humble in the
closet ; if it be conscious of its own superiority to its
contemporaries, it will be none the less conscious of
its inferiority to its own ideals.   The intimate union
of pride and of humility, which is characteristic of all
genius, and pre-eminently sincere in it, can never be
understood by the world at large.

Flaubert, as we know, corrected, effaced, recon-

structed, erased and altered every line of his text a
hundred times, in careless dissatisfaction with himself;
but when an editor of a review asked him to make
some corrections in the proof of St Julian Hospitador,
he haughtily replied to the meddler : ' *Des corrections ?*
—*j'en donne quelquefois, mais je n'en fais jamais!* '
Inexorable self-scourger in his study or his studio, the
man of genius is high-mettled and arrogant as an
hidalgo before interference. How should the fool
understand this?—the fool who deems himself perfect
when strutting before his mirror, but is downcast
before the first mocking glance or ridiculing word
which he encounters in the public street !

Humanity loves to scoff, and say that genius is
human. No doubt it is; but its humanity is always
of a different kind to that of ordinary men. The
nightingale is classified by naturalists amongst the
tribe of the Sparrows, in the class of the Finches ; but
this fact does not make the nightingale only a
sparrow, or only a finch. The nightingale sees life
and nature very differently to the sparrow, though his
physical organisation may, in some respects, resemble
his kinsman's. It is one thing to sit on the housetops
and drink rinsings from the gutter, and another to sit
on a myrtle bough and drink dew from the heart of a
rose. How shall those to whom the rinsings are
sweet be able to judge those for whom the rose is
chalice-bearer ?

In a recent monograph upon his friend Meissonier,
Alexandre Dumas has quoted some petulant and
childish sayings of the great painter which would
have been better left in oblivion. Dumas prefaces
them by the phrase ' J'ai entendu Meissonier dire,

mais peut-être, il est vrai, ne le disait-il qu'à moi :
in these last words, '*ne le disait-il qu'à moi*,' lies the
whole gist of the matter, in these few words are contained the confession of the consciousness which
should have preserved Meissonier's impetuous and
unconsidered self-revelations from being, after his
death, made public by his friend. It is just these
things which are said only to us, which are said
perhaps foolishly, perhaps hastily, perhaps stupidly,
but in any way said in entire good faith, and in the
conviction of the good faith of the confidant, which
should never be repeated, above all when the ground
is closed over the speakers of them. It will be said
that there is nothing in this recollection of Meissonier
which is in any way to his discredit. There is not.
Yet it is none the less a violation of confidence ; and in
a sense it dwarfs the stature of him. One of the chief
characteristics of genius is an extreme youthfulness of
feeling and of impulse, often also of expression ; the
great artist is always in one side of his nature a child.
But this fact, which is so lovable and engaging in him
in his lifetime, makes him continually, in his careless
and confidential utterances, say what is natural, and
may even be beautiful in its spontaneity and suitability
to the moment of its expression, but which loses its
colour, its light, its charm, as a dried and pressed
flower loses them when it is reproduced after death in
the rigidity of type.

Taine set a fine example in his will when he enjoined on his heirs to burn all the documents in
which he had written down all he had heard from his
contemporaries. The rose should be always hung
before the door wherever two or three are gathered

together in familiar intercourse, and the inquisitive, censorious, malignant world is listening cunningly at the keyhole. The world will not go away for the rose ; but those within should enforce respect for its symbol, and should stuff up the keyhole.

I once knew and liked for several years a diplomatist who was very popular in society. He was often with me, and one day he unfortunately told me that it was his habit to write down every night, no matter how late it might be when he went home, the record of everything witty, or interesting, or singular, that he had heard during the day, and the names of all the persons whom he had met and with whom he had conversed. 'I have done this,' he added, 'ever since I was an unpaid *attaché*, and these volumes, which are many, as you may imagine, will not be published until the time designated to my executors in my will.' Ever after this confession from him I saw him with much less pleasure ; these bulky volumes, though unseen, cast their grim shadow over the present and the future ; I never again laughed and talked with him without the recollection that he was treasuring up the nonsense I spoke or repeated to write it down in black and white before he allowed himself to sleep. The thought was a ghost at every intellectual banquet at which he and I met. I wanted to call out to our companions,

'There's a chiel amang you takin' notes.'

As he was a man who had his *petite entrée* into the arcana of politics, and was personally acquainted with the most distinguished people of Europe, he must have burned a good deal of post-midnight oil over his nightly chronicle, and I wonder he could keep awake to make it.

He died some years since, and of those voluminous records there is nothing said in the press as yet. No doubt, however, they will see the light some day ; and some heir or heirs will make a round sum of money out of them. There is a kind of treason in this habit of committing to paper for ultimate publication what is said by those around us. If the matter be emended and emasculated when printed, it loses all interest ; if published verbatim, the publication constitutes a betrayal. Social intercourse is surely based on the tacit assumption that what is said in it is said under cover of the white flag of mutual trust. I do not think that we have any right whatever to make any kind of private conversation public. The motive for doing so can never be a very high one. There is, no doubt, a great temptation in the wish to tell what we know about a friend whose character we see was unknown or misunderstood by the world in general, even probably by his intimate associates ; but I doubt if we have the right to do so. If he revealed his natural inner self more completely to us than to others, it was no doubt because we inspired him with a more complete confidence or sympathy than did others. Shall that confidence or that sympathy be abused or betrayed by any man or woman of common honour?

It is a fact which is to be regretted that the faculty of inspiring confidence is, unfortunately, often allied to an utter faithlessness in keeping it. Those who most attract it are often those who most betray it. The sympathy which draws out our secrets is frequently united to considerable treachery in using them. Even those who are in many ways faithful and sincere betray after death those who trusted them in life, by revelations of their correspondence, either intentional or careless.

'Cachez votre vie: étalez votre esprit,' is a wise counsel; but it is this which the world will not permit if it can by any torment prevent it. He who has once allowed his wit to shine, and dazzle the eyes of his contemporaries, is expected to live his life for ever afterwards with open doors.

People who are famous are invariably accused of being self-conscious, reserved, monosyllabic, lacking in candour, in expansiveness, in inclination to converse. What more natural than that they should be so, since they know that their most intimate companion may not be able to resist the temptation of recording and retailing everything they say? If they speak as they feel, they are accused of 'giving themselves away,' as the English slang phrases it; if they be as reserved and as silent as it is possible to be without offence to society, they are accused of *morgue*, of vanity, of arrogance. In either case, whatever they do say, whether it be much or be little, will be certainly exaggerated, misrepresented, and disliked. Meissonier may, in a weak moment, wish he were Fortuny; Tennyson may, in an irritable hour, prefer money to fame; and each may say so to a trusted companion. But it is hard that the evanescent, unwise desire should be soberly published many years after in each case by a hearer who was deemed a friend.

We are none of us, perhaps, as loyal as we ought

to be in speech. We are too thoughtless in what we repeat; and many, for sake of an epigram or a *jeu de mot*, sacrifice the higher duties of respect for confidence and silence on it.' But speech may have the excuse of unpremeditation, haste, the contagion of conversation going on around. The indiscretions of written and of printed words share none of these excuses. Even if written in hurry or in carelessness, there is leisure enough when a proof sheet is received, between its reception and its publication, for all such revelations to be effaced. Have we a right to make public private conversations? I do not consider that we have. Intercourse, at all events the pleasure of intercourse, reposes on the tacit condition that its privacy is intangible. Intimate correspondence does the same. In letters we give hostages to our friends. It should be understood that such hostages are not to be led, like captives, into the public market-place and sold.

In the many memories of intimacy with Alfred Tennyson which have been published since his death, few would, I think, have pleased a man so reluctant to be observed and commented on as was he. The fulsome adulation would scarcely have sufficed to reconcile him to the cruel dissection.

Famous people, like obscure ones, do not weigh every syllable they speak; and the former pay heavily for imprudent utterance, whilst the latter sin scotfree because nobody cares a straw what they say or do not say. Tennyson, in an imprudent moment, said once to Henry Irving that Shelley had no sense of humour. It is quite true that Shelley had not: his life would have been brighter and happier if he had been able to laugh oftener ; and it is exceedingly unfair to Tennyson to twist this statement of an actual fact into a depreciation of Shelley to his own self-praise. Even if he implied that he were the greater poet of the two, should a friend deride this, should a trusted companion record it ?

Mr Knowles relates how Tennyson, speaking of his habit of composing verses which he never wrote down as he sat over the winter's fire, added, ' How many hundreds of fine lines went up the chimney and vanished !' The world cries out, ' What ! did he call his own verses fine ?' Why should he not? He must have known that he enriched the English language with scores of fine lines, as I suppose he must have known that he made many with false quantities, which halt painfully. But are these careless, natural phrases, utterances which should be produced in print? Nothing can divest such *post-mortem* revelations of a suspicion of treachery. They suggest the note-book of the diplomatist, in which at nightfall were recorded all the witty sayings and careless confidences heard during the daytime.

Mr Knowles, who admired Tennyson extremely, and lived for many years in his close intimacy, puts into print the saying of Tennyson that he wished he could have had the money which his books had brought without the nuisance of the fame which accompanied it. This was not an heroic speech, though it might be a natural one. It was probably a wrathful ebullition excited by the irritation of public comment and the prying impertinence of public curiosity. But it is the kind of speech which is never intended for reproduction in print. We all have these moments of ungrateful impatience with our lot. The king wishes himself in the hovel, the hind wishes himself on the throne. Whoso gathers the laurel longs for the cowslip, he who has the field flowers sighs for the myrtle and the bays. But it is not the place of a bosom friend to stereotype for all time the reproach of Fortune's favourites to the magnificent caprices of Fortune. Certainly Tennyson, having been compelled to choose, would have chosen the poverty and fame of Homer or of Cervantes rather than a life of inglorious ease and obscure eating of good dinners. The imperishable record in print, of a passing mood of irritability in which he said otherwise, is therefore a cruel injustice done to him.

It is impossible for the ordinary mind, which is usually dense of perception and greedy of observation, to attempt to measure or conceive in any degree the unsupportable torment to a sensitive temper and an exalted intelligence of the mosquito swarm of inquisitive interrogators and commentators; of the exaggeration, the misrepresentation, the offensive calumnies, and the still more offensive admiration, which are the daily penalty of all greatness. The adoring American, perched staring in the pear tree outside the dining-room window, may well have embittered to Tennyson the meats and wines of his dinner-table within. If he had got up from his table and shot the spy, such a pardonable impulse should certainly have been considered justifiable homicide. That because a man has done something higher, better, more, beautiful than his fellows, he is therefore to be subjected without resistance to their curiosity and comment, is a premiss so intolerable that it should not be permitted to be advanced in any decent society. The interviewer is the vilest spawn of the most ill-bred age which the world has yet seen. If he be received, when he intrudes, with the toe of the boot, he has but his fitting reception.

There has been lately published the following personal description of a great writer whom I will not especially designate. It runs as follows : 'The first impression one gets is of a small man with large feet, walking as if for a wager, arms swinging hither and thither, and fingers briskly playing imaginary tunes in the air as he goes. Then, as the eccentric shape comes nearer, one is aware of a stubby beard and peeping eyes expressive of mingled distrust and aversion ; a hideous hat is clapped down on the broad brow, which hat, when lifted, displays a bald expanse of skull bearing no sort of resemblance whatever to the counterfeit (*sic*) presentiments of Apollo ; and yet, incongruous though it seems, this little vacuous, impatient, querulous being is no other than—' And then there is named one of the greatest masters of language whom the world has ever owned.

Yet who, having read this infamous portrait of physical defects, whether it be truth or libel, can ever again entirely divest his memory of it, can ever wholly prevent its arising in odious ridicule between him and his rapturous sense of the perfect music of a great style ? Shakespeare cursed those who would not let his bones alone ; the living genius may with equal justice curse those who will not let alone his living form and features. There are only two classes of persons who may be certain of seeing every physical fault or deformity or affliction in face or

E

form brutally written down in print : they are the
man of genius in the reports of his contemporaries,
and the escaped criminal on the handbills and search-
warrants of the police. Renan and Arton receive
exactly the same measure.

The vulgar, the Herr Omnes of Luther, cannot
comprehend the hatred, the loathing of observation
and comment, which are of the very essence of the
poetic temperament. Yet it is strange to think that
being mobbed can be agreeable to anyone. The
sense of being pursued by incessant curiosity, as often
as not a merely malignant curiosity, must poison the
hours of life to the proud and sensitive nature. Such
curiosity existed, no doubt, in the days of Ovid, in
the days of Alkibiades ; but modern inquisitiveness
is far worse, being armed with all the modern powers
to torture. The intolerable Kodak, the intolerable
interviewer, the artifices of the press, the typewriter,
the telegraph, the telephone, the greedy, indelicate,
omnivorous mind of the modern public—all contribute to make of celebrity a Gehenna.

Creation is the paradise of the artist or poet ;
sympathy, if it be also true, is balm to him ; for the
opinion of others he will never greatly care if his lips
have been truly touched with the coal from the altar,
yet the sense of his influence over them will be welcome to him ; but the espionage of the multitude will
be always to him irritating as mosquito bites, pestilent
as a swarm of termites, darkening like a locust flight
the face of the sun.

It is hard to think that one who has an illustrious
name cannot idly gossip with an intimate friend
without every careless word being stereotyped. One

is grateful to Mr Knowles for telling us that Tennyson declared he would shake his fists in the face of Almighty God if He, etc., etc. One rejoices to know of this outburst of honest indignation at the unpitied sufferings of the helpless and the harmless, this grand flinging of the phylacteries in the face of a hypocritical and egotistic world. At the same time it is surely impossible to admit that such a spontaneous and impassioned expression of emotion ought, by any hearer of it, to have been, in cold blood, put on record and produced in print?

Poor dead singer of Ida and Œnone! The ruthless inquisitors who poisoned his life still pursue him even beyond the cold waters of the Styx! There is something infinitely pathetic in the knowledge of how, all his life long, Tennyson endeavoured to avoid the intrusion of the crowd, and of how utterly useless all his wishes and endeavours were, and how those whom he trusted and confided in, bring out the dead children of his spoken thoughts naked in the sight of the multitude whom he shunned.

The confidential utterances of great men and women should no more be desecrated by being told to the public than tears and kisses should be profaned by the publicity of a railway station.

The general reader can no more understand why Tennyson suffered so intensely at seeing a chestnut tree felled in full flower than they can understand the course in the heavens of Argol or Altair. To spread out before them these delicate, intricate, bleeding fibres of the soul is to slay Pegasus and Philomel to make a workhouse meal.

Mr Knowles alleges that it is necessary for him

and other intimate friends of Tennyson to say all they thought of him, and repeat all he said, because a similar record of Shakespeare's conversations would be so precious a treasure to the world. This, also, is a questionable premiss. Shakespeare, happy in so much, was happiest of all in the obscurity in which his personality is sheltered ; and the world is to be congratulated that it knows too little of the man to squabble and dwarf and disfigure him to the detriment of his works, as it does Byron and Shelley. What the man is matters so little. Psychology is but another name for curiosity, envy, or *dénigremené*. Whether the orchid grow on a rotten tree, or the lily on a dunghill, affects not the beauty of the orchid or the fragrance of the lily. What Horace was, or was not, at the Augustan Court cannot touch the exquisite grace of his style, the lovely lines of his pictures in words. The more we look at any writer the less we are likely to do justice to his creations, because his personality will exercise upon us either a great attraction or a great repulsion. It would be better for all works if, like Cologne Cathedral, they were without known progenitors.

Could Dante Rossetti ever have dreamed that Mr Leyland would preserve the poor, pathetic little note asking for the gift of more wine in his last illness, which Mr Val. Prinsep saw fit to publish in the *Art Journal* of September 1892 ? If we may not trust our most intimate friends with our necessities, in whom can we confide ? The whole of this aforesaid correspondence of Rossetti was never intended for, nor is it fitted for, publication. The general world has a right to see any artist's completed work, and judge it

as they may choose to do, but they have no right to
be made acquainted with the hesitations, the self-
torment, the fluctations, the depression, the exultation, which preceded its birth.   These are the
ecstasies and the agonies which precede all gestation
and parturition, and are not for public exhibition.
Mr Leyland, loving Rossetti well, should have burned
all these letters before, or immediately after, the
artist's death.   Mr Leyland was a man who knew his
generation, and must have known the use which
would be made of them.   If a friend grant me a
favour, and afterwards blab of that favour to our
common acquaintances, I should prefer that such a
favour had never been accorded.   I think that most
people will agree with this feeling.   Yet reticence
concerning favours done is not common in our times.
Such reticence ought to be held the simplest obligation of honour ; but the majority of persons do not so
regard it.   There is hardly a letter of any length ever
written in which there are not some sentences liable
to misconstruction, or open to various readings.   It
is grossly unfair to place any letter before those who
are not in the possession of its key ; that key which
can alone lie in an intimate knowledge of its writer's
circumstances and temperament.   If Rossetti were
not rich enough to buy the wine he wanted in his
weakness, the shame is not his, but that of the world
which left him poor.   To think that he was too poor
even to ever see Italy is an intolerable disgrace to his
contemporaries.   He would have been wiser to have
left his patrons and to have lived in Italy on a black
crust and a plate of bean soup.

    If the man of genius amass wealth, he is accused of

avarice or of mercenary sale of his own talent.. If he remain poor, or be in trouble, no language can sufficiently condemn his extravagance, his improvidence, his immorality. If he live with any kind of splendour, it is display and profligacy ; if he endeavour to avoid remark, it is meanness, hauteur or poverty.

Men and women of genius when they have money are too generous with it, and when they have it not are too careless about the lack of it. Shakespeare, we are told, had the prudence to put his money together and to buy houses and lands, with shrewd eye to the main chance ; but this is, after all, mere supposition on the part of posterity. We know so little of the circumstances of his life that, for aught we can tell, he may have had some sharp-eyed, true-hearted friend or factor, who thus transmuted the poet's loose coins into solid fields and freeholds, as George Eliot had behind her George Lewis. I cannot believe that Titania's laureate ever quarrelled over deeds of copyhold and questions of fees and betterments with the burgesses and notaries of Stratford - upon - Avon. More likely, far, that he was lying in the sun, dreaming, deep cradled in cowslips and ladysmocks, as his winged verses flew up with the bees into the budding lime boughs overhead, whilst some trusty friend or brother did battle in his name with the chafferers and the scriveners in the little town. And when all was settled, and the deeds of transfer only wanted signature and seal, that trusty go-between would shout across the meadows to waken Will from his day-dream, and Will would lazily arise and come across the grass, with the pollen of the bees and the fragrant yellow dust of the cowslips on his clothes, and, with his sweet, serene smile, would scrawl his name to parchments which he scarcely even read. That is, I would take my oath, how the stores of Shakespeare increased, and how New Place became his. Pembroke's friend and Rosalind's creator never cared much for lucre, I am sure ; for land he might care, because he loved England : he loved her fields, her woods, her streams, and he saw them as her sons can never see them now, uninjured and undimmed, the Lenten lilies growing tall beneath the untrimmed hedges of hazel and hawthorn, the water meadows spreading broad and fair, without a curl of smoke in sight, save that which rose from the cottage hearths. Elizabethan England was meadow where it was not coppice, park where it was not forest, heathery moorland where it was not reedy mere. It was natural that Shakespeare should care to call his own some portion of that beautiful leafy kingdom of his birth.

Even so Scott loved his Scottish soil, and Tennyson cared to own Farringford and Hazelmere. Even so George Sand's last dying words were of the trees of Nohant. Passion and pleasure and fame and love were in those last moments naught to her, but the green, fresh, dewy leafage of dead summers was still dear.

The psychologist Lombroso, in a recent essay, which must fill the *bourgeois* breast with exultation, finding that it is not possible for him to deny the mental fecundity of genius, denies its physical fertility, and endeavours to prove his assertion, after the customary method of scientists, by avoiding and omitting every fact which would in any manner

tell against his theory. Evidence when manipulated
by the scientist is like the colt when it issues, docked
and clipped, from its training stable. Laying down
the proposition that precocity is atavistic, founded on
the declaration of the biologist, Dr Delaunay, that it is
a sign of inferiority, he cites the marvellous precocity
of Raffaelle, Pascal, Mozart, Victor Hugo, Mirabeau,
Dante, Handel, Calderon, Tasso, and many others,
who prove, on the contrary, that precocity is the
sign of splendour, strength and durability of genius.
He remarks that precocity is a mark of insignificance,
and that the small and low organism develops with
much greater rapidity than the higher order ! Were
we not used to the pompous self-contradictions of
Science, we should be surprised to see a characteristic
of so many great minds pronounced to be a defect
and a deformity ; it is certainly only a scientist who
would dream of classing Raffaelle, Dante, Mozart,
Hugo, amongst the lesser organisms.

The whole argument is built on the same quagmire
of illogical assertion and false deduction. He first lays
down as an axiom that men of genius are physically
sterile, and supports it by the strange and curiously
incorrect assertion that Shakespeare and Milton had
no posterity ! He proceeds to quote the saying of
La Bruyère : 'Ces hommes n'ont ni ancêtres ni pos-
térités ; ils forment eux-seuls toute une descendance.'
Now, as regards ancestry, it is clear that La Bruyère
spoke figuratively : he did not and could not mean
that men of genius have no progenitors : he meant
that who their progenitors were did not matter to the
world which cared only for themselves ; in a similar
way he spoke of their descendants, not as actually

non-existent, but as counting for nothing beside the superior creation of their works.

Amongst the sterile *célibataires* Lombroso oddly enough includes Voltaire and Alfieri, whose loves and liaisons were famous and numerous. He entirely ignores Victor Hugo, whose philoprogenitiveness was so excessive as to be absurd ; the extreme affection for their offspring of Tennyson and Renan, of George Sand and of Juliette Adam, of Millias and of Meissonier, of Mario and of Grisi, and of countless others whose names are famous and whose affections were or are most ardent. The offspring publicly recognised by man or woman is by no means necessarily the sole offspring of either. Allegra is not mentioned beside Ada in Burke's Peerage. Natural children frequently are not allowed to know even their own parentage ; a woman may have children whom she does not openly acknowledge ; a man may have children of whose birth even he knows nothing. It is not every celebrated woman who has the maternal courage of George Sand, nor every celebrated man who has the paternal tenderness of Shelley.

Lombroso confuses in a most unscientific manner the passion of love and the bond of marriage. Because Michael Angelo says that art is wife enough for him, Lombroso supposes that no passion, good or evil, ever moved him. The fact that a man or woman has not married does not prove that they have had no amours : the probability is that their ardour and caprice in love have withheld them from the captivity of a legal union, which is usually the tomb of love. Everything which disturbs the odd conclusion to which it has pleased him to come is put aside and left out by a writer whose treatise pretends to be based on an inexorable accuracy. He carefully omits all reference to the men of old who would, almost without exception, disprove his theory. The three greatest of these are surely Mahomet, Alexander and Julius Cæsar : all this triad were famous for sensual indulgence almost without limit. So far as the fact may be considered to honour genius, its alliance with the joys of voluptuous passions is fully established, and no ingenuity in paradox of a perverse hater of it can contravene the fact. As for the poets, from Catullus to Burns, they rise in their graves and laugh in the face of the biologist. Sterile ? They ? As well call sterile the red clover which yields its fecundating pollen to the bee in the glad sunlight of a summer day.

The great singer called Mario was a man of genius in every way, apart from the art in which he was unsurpassed : yet, he was a singularly handsome man, and possessed of magical seduction for women. Of the Spanish poet Zorilla, for whose recent death all Spanish women wept, the same may be said. Longfellow was very handsome, and his life was lovely, noble, and harmonious, from his youth to his grave. The physical beauty of Washington is well known, yet his genius cannot be contested. Vandyke had extreme physical beauty ; Raffaelle also ; the painters have nearly always been conspicuous for personal beauty, from Leonardo to Millais and Leighton. Gladstone has very fine features and a magnificent constitution ; his physical strength is wonderful, yet his intellect has always been at full stretch, like a racing greyhound. The personal beauty and fine stature of Tennyson were accompanied by the most

keen intellectual ardour, extant until the very latest
day of his life. The beauty of Milton and of Goethe
has become traditional in their respective countries.
Wellington and Marlborough were singularly handsome men. Napoleon was a man of short stature, but
his face had a classic beauty which resisted even death,
as may be seen in the mask taken from his dead
features at St Helena. Take Lamartine ; place his
verse where you will, it is impossible to deny his
genius, the genius of intense poetic sympathy and
insight, of eloquence, of magical music of utterance, of
comprehension of all creatures which live and suffer ;
he himself was his finest poem, and as to his wonderful physical beauty there can be no dispute. Of three
typical men of genius of modern times take Shakespeare, Goethe and Henri Quatre ; all were of much
beauty of person, and masculine vigour was not lacking in any ; in the two latter it was even excessive.
The hero of Arques and Ivry was the lover of more
fair women than peopled the harem of Sardanapalus.
Yet he had supreme genius ; the genius of command,
of wit, of intuition, of magnetic charm over the minds
and wills and hearts of men ; a charm which has been
stronger than death, and has kept the fascination of
his memory green throughout the length and breadth
of France. Many more similar examples might be
quoted. These, however, suffice to prove the inexacti-
tude of the envious calumnies cast upon genius by
Lombroso, who actually asserts that genius is never
separated from physical degeneracy, and that the
splendour of the brain is always paid for by atrophy
of other organs ! Were this true, the wretched, deformed, stunted creatures, the arrest of whose physical

development is artificially obtained by the most cruel torture, and constitutes a trade in the Cevennes and the Pyrenees, would all of them become Napoleons, Goethes, Byrons, Mussets, Racines and Bismarcks. The manufacture of cripples would be the manufacture of heroes and poets! The favourite theory of scientists that genius is *caused* by physical imperfection is manifestly untrue, and grossly calumnious. It means, if it means anything, that the physically imperfect creature is the intellectually perfect; that the scrofulous and hunchbacked dwarf is the light-giver of the world, the Apollo Citharædus of the arts. What facts bear out such a theory?

Equally calumnious and false is the conclusion by Lombroso, that the man of genius (like the madman) is born, lives and dies, *cold, solitary, invisible.* A more abominable libel was never penned by mediocrity on greatness. The sweet, bright humour of Scott, buoyant even beneath woe and bodily pain; the gay, delightful kindliness of Molière, the cheerful, serene philosophies of Montaigne, the superb resistance to calamity of Cervantes, the playful, indulgent, affectionate temper of Thackeray, the noble tranquillity in adversity of Milton, the happy whimsical humour of Horace, the calm and fruitful leisure of Suetonius, the adoration of Nature of all the poets, from Theocritus to Lecomte de Lisle—all these and a thousand others arise to memory in refutation of this ignoble libel. Who held that the saddest things on earth were—

> ' Un cage sans oiseaux, une ruche sans abeilles,
> Une maison sans enfans?'

Victor Hugo: the master of one of the most fertile,

puissant and imaginative minds ever known on earth. That genius seeks solitude is natural : it is only the fool who is afraid of his own company; the meditations and intellectual memories of genius must always be more delightful to it than the babble of society.

The commerce and conversation of the majority of persons is wearisome, trivial, dull ; it is not wonderful that one who can commune in full harmony of thought with Nature, and with the wisdom of old, turns from the common babble of the common herd, and seeks the shelter of the library, or the silence of the forest and the moor. But such an one will always give more human sympathy than he can ever receive. None can see into his soul ; but the souls of others are laid bare to him. To others he is a mystery which they fear ; but others are to him as children whom he pities. If their folly and deadness of heart arouse his scorn, he yet weeps for them, because they know not what they do. They cannot hear, as he hears, the sigh in the leaves of the fallen tree, the woe in the cry of the widowed bird, the voices of the buried nations calling from the unseen tombs : no, in that sense he is alone, as the seer is alone and the prophet ; but this loneliness comes not from the coldness of his own heart, but from the poverty of the hearts of other men. Who dares to say that those who alone can put into speech the emotions of a humanity, in itself dumb and helpless, are incapable of feeling those emotions which without them would find neither utterance nor interpreter.

Lombroso speaks exultingly of the cruelty to women of Musset, Byron, Carlyle and others ; he has evidently no conception of the intense irritation roused in sensitive natures by uncongenial and enforced companionship. Jane Carlyle was a woman of fine wit and character, but she had no tact and little patience, and her sharp retorts must have been as thorns in the flesh of her bilious and melancholy Saul, as his uncouthness and ill-breeding must have been cruel trials to her. But this was no fault of either of them : it was the fault of that sad mistake, so common in the world, of an ill-assorted marriage, in which the prisoners suffered only the more because they were, in their different ways, of fine character, with a sense of duty so acute in each that it was a torture to both alike. What Lombroso calls the brutality of Carlyle was probably little else than the morbid gloom caused by a diseased liver, this disease in turn caused by the constraint and asphyxiation of a town life in a small house to a man born of hardy, outdoor, rustic stock, and farmed to breathe the strong, keen air of solitary Scottish moors and hills, to be braced by storm and sunshine, to battle with snow and wind and rain. The terrible folly which drives men of talent into cities, and leave them only the vitiated air of close and crowded streets, of feverish gatherings, and of unhealthy club-houses, is the origin of that alliance, so often seen in the present age, between the gifted mind and the suffering body, or the restless nerves, of a *névrosé*, of a hypochondriac, or of a bilious diabetic.

Lombroso, in the malignant spitefulness with which the scientists throw mud and stones at all genius, calls Byron a *Rachitique*, on account of his deformed foot ; but when we remember Byron's splendid swim-

ming powers, his endurance in the saddle, his passion
for the mountains and the sea, his heroic calmness on
his lonely deathbed, we must, if we are sincere, admit
that this *Rachitique*, even apart from all his superb
genius, was a man of no common courage and no
common force, and that, whatever might be at birth
the physical weakness accompanying his great physical beauty, he had known· how to make himself the
equal of the strongest even in outdoor sports. When
we think of that great beauty before which women
went down as corn before the flash of the reaping-
hook, of the incomparable romance of that life, passing from the crowds of St James's to the pine solitudes
of Ravenna, from the adulation of Courts to the
silence of Alp and ocean, from the darksome glens
and braes of Scotland to the azure light on the
Hellespont and the Adrian Sea—when we think of
its marvellous compass brought within the short span
of thirty-six years, of its god-like powers, of its surpassing gifts, of its splendour of song, of wit, of
melody, of passion, and of inspiration, of its tragic
close, which broke off the laurel bough in its green
prime, as Apollo would have it broken—when we
think of this life, I say, it is easy to understand why
its effulgence has been the mark for every petty
malignity and jealous mediocrity ever since the light
of the sun died down at Missolonghi.

Byron's must ever remain the most ideal, the most
splendid, the most varied life which ever incarnated in
itself the genius of man and the gifts of the gods : what
joy, then, to the petty and the envious to point to his
club foot, and to assure us he was *Rachitique!* The
puling versifiers who spend their lifetime in elaborating

artificial sonnets based on early Italian methods,
straining, refining, paring, altering, transforming, trying to replace by effort all which is lacking to them
in inspiration, may well be unable to comprehend
aught of that fiery fury of scorn and invective, of
that Niagara-like rush of thought and word and
imagery, which made verse as natural an utterance to
Byron as the torrent of its song is natural to the
nightingale in the months of spring. To the grand
verse of Byron there may be rivals, there may be
superiors; but to the poetry of his life there is no
equal in any other life. What greater, more unpardonable sin can he have in the sight of mediocrity?

I lately saw a tourist of small stature, mean appear-
ance, and awkward gesture, criticising unfavourably
the attitude of the beautiful Mercury in the Vatican
Rotonda. I was irresistibly reminded of certain versifiers and newspaper essayists of the present moment
criticising Byron!

Lombroso asserts that 'the man of genius has only
contempt for other men of genius ; he is offended by
all praise not given to himself; the dominant feeling
of a man of genius, or even of erudition, is hatred and
scorn for all other men who possess, or approach the
possession of genius or talent.' A greater libel was
never penned. It is natural that those who are
masters of their art should be less easy to please, less
ignorant of its demands and beauties, than the crowd
can be. The great writer, the great artist, the great
composer, can scarcely fail to feel some disdain for
the facility with which the public is satisfied, the
fatuity with which it accepts the commonplace, the

second-rate, the imitation, the mere catch-penny, as true and original creation. But this scorn for the mediocre, which is inseparable from all originality and is its right and privilege, does not for a moment preclude the ardent sympathy, the joyous recognition with which genius will salute the presence of kindred genius. What of the friendship of Coleridge and Wordsworth, of Byron and Shelley, of Flaubert and George Sand, of Shakespeare and Ben Jonson? Scarce a year ago two illustrious men conversed with sympathy and friendship under the green leaves by the waters of Annecy. Philippe Berthelet narrates how 'sous les vieux noyers de Talloires ils discutèrent pour la première fois de leur vie, Renan défendant son cher Lamartine, et Taine son poëte préféré Musset; je garde un pieux souvenir des nobles paroles de ces deux grands hommes qu'il m'a été donné d'entendre ce soir de Septembre sur le bord du lac limpide, au pied de la Tournette couronnée de neiges.'

The public likes inferior production; as a rule prefers it, because it understands it more easily; and this preference may irritate the supreme artist into a burst of wrath. Berlioz gave the *Damnation de Faust* to empty benches, and his Titanic disdain of his contemporaries for their preference of weaker men has been justified by the verdict of the present generation. But this sentiment of scorn is as far removed from the petty malignity of envy and injustice as the fury of the tempest amongst the Alps or Andes is unlike the sputtering of a candle guttering in a tin sconce. To the poet to see the poetaster crowned; to the great man to see his miserable imitator accepted as his equal; to the planet on high to know that the street

F

lamp below is thought his rival, must ever be offensive. But this offence is just, and has grandeur in it ; it is no more meanness and jealousy than the planet is the gaspipe or the Alpine storm the candle.

To the great artist it is a great affront to see the imitator of himself, the thief, the dauber, the mimic, the mediocre, accepted as an artist by the world. He is entitled to resent the affront and to scourge the offender. The intolerance of genius for mediocrity is called unkindness : it is no more unkind than the sentence of the judge on the criminal. In our time the material facilities given to production have multiplied mediocrity as heat multiplies carrion flies ; it should have no quarter shown to it ; it is a ravaging pest.

Cheap printing makes writers of thousands who would be more fittingly employed in stitching shoes or digging ditches ; and the assistance of photography makes painters or draughtsmen of thousands who would be more harmlessly occupied whitewashing sheds or carding wool. Genius is as rare as ever it was in all the arts ; but the impudent pretensions of nullity to replace and represent it increase with every year, because it finds readier · acceptance from the ever-increasing ignorance of a universally educated public. The men of genius who do exist do not say this loudly enough or often enough : they are afraid to look unkind and to create enemies. It is not excellence which is malignant, envious, slanderous, mean : it is inferiority ; inferiority dressed in the cheap garment of ill-fitting success.

There is a draughtsman who is very eminent in our time, and whose drawings have brought him in alike celebrity and wealth. He is esteemed one of the first artists in black-and-white of the century. Yet he never draws a line of any figure without resorting to his immense collection of photographs of all kinds and conditions of persons, in all attitudes and in all costumes, whence he selects whatever he may want to reproduce. This habit may perhaps not impair his skill as a draughtsman; but it certainly makes him a mere imitator, a mere copyist, and robs his works of all spontaneity, originality and sincerity. To draw from a photograph is mere copying, mere cheating; it is not art at all. Yet this popular draughtsman has not the least shame or hesitation in avowing his methods; nor do his public or his critics appear to see anything to censure or regret in them. If the true artist, who is sincere and original in all his creations, who draws from life, and would no more employ a camera than he would pick a pocket, feels, and expresses the contempt which he feels, for the draughtsman who is dependent on photographs, he is not moved either by hostility or jealousy, but by a wholesome and most just disdain. It is a disdain with which the general public can have little sympathy, because they cannot estimate the quality of the offence which excites it.

To the creator, whether of prose, of poem, of melody, picture, or statue, who is sincere in all he creates, to whom conscious imitation would have all the baseness of a forgery, and to whom sincerity and originality are the essence of creative talent, the fraud of imitation disgusts and offends as it cannot do the mere outsider. Such disgust, such offence, are no more envy or jealousy than the sublime fury of the storming-party is the secret stabbing of the hired bravo.

Oh, the obscure! the vile obscure! what shafts dipped in gall will they not let fly from the dusky parlour in which they sit and look with envious scowl out on the distant splendour of great lives!

The sweetest singer who ever sang on the classic Tyrrhene shore—Shelley, who soared with the sky-lark and suffered with the demi-god—Shelley leaves unhappily behind him a piteous little letter telling his friend Williams, in Dublin, of his poverty, and asking for the loan of five-and-twenty pounds; and this poor little letter is basely preserved and is sold by auction in London in the month of March of last year for the sum of eleven sovereigns! *O beati insipientes!* who cares whether you borrow five-and-twenty pounds, or five-and-twenty pence, or five-and-twenty thousand? Who cares to keep your humble request, your timid confession? Who cares whether you got what you craved, or were left to die of hunger? You, the mediocre, the commonplace, the incapable, are left in peace; but the sorry, carking, humiliating need of the beautiful boy-singer, whose name is blessed for all time, is dragged into the auction-mart and bid for rabidly by the curious! What joy for you, you well-fed, broad-bellied, full-pursed hordes of the common-place, to think that this sensitive plant shivered and sickened under the vulgar hand of dun and bailiff, and withered in the sandy waste of want! He could write down the music of the lark, and hear the laughter of the fairies, and paint the changing glories of the sea, and suffer with the fallen Titan as with the trodden flower—but he was once in sore need of five-

and-twenty pounds! *O beati insipientes!* Here lie your triumphs and your revenge. Clasp your fat palms above your ample paunch, and grin as you embrace your banker's pass-book. Take heed to keep that little letter of the poet of the 'Prometheus' safe under glass for all time, to comfort the jealous pains of the millions of nonentities whom you will continue to procreate until the end of time! Such are the consolations of inferiority.

Genius offends by its unlikeness to the general; it scorns their delights, their views, their creeds, their aspirations; it is at once much simpler and much more profound than they; it suffices to itself in a manner which,·to the multitude, seems arrogance; the impersonal is always much more absorbing to it than the personal; there are qualities in it at once childlike and godlike, which offend the crowd at once by their ignorance and by their wisdom. In a word, it is apart from them; and they know that, they feel that, and they cannot forgive its unlikeness.

O Beati Insipientes! Unwatched, you eat and drink and work and play; unchronicled are your errors and your follies; would you weep, you may weep in peace; would you take a country walk, no spy, notebook in hand, will lurk in the hedges; when you pour out your trivial nonsense in the ear of a friend, he will not treasure it up to turn it into printer's copy as soon as you shall be cold in your coffin.

O Beati Insipientes! You know not what safety, what peace, what comfort are gained for you by your mantle of obscurity. You know not, and you would not believe though angels and archangels descended

to tell it you, that the splendour of the sunlight of
fame is darkened for ever to those whose path lies
through it by the shadow which follows, mimicking,
prying, listening, grinning, girding, slobbering, eagerly
watching for a false step, cruelly counting the thorns
trodden amidst the flowers—that shadow which dogs
without mercy the whole of a life, and thrusts its prying fingers through the cere-clothes of death, that
shadow of merciless and malign curiosity which
follows genius as the assassin followed the fair youth
Crichton through the streets of Mantua : the crime
of Crichton being to excel !

CITIES OF ITALY

W HATEVER may be the opinion of Europe as
to the political advantages accruing to it
from the independence of Italy, it must be mournfully
confessed that the losses to art and to history through
it are greater than any which could have been caused
by centuries of neglect or long years of hostile occupation and devastating war. It is scarcely to be
measured, indeed, what those losses are ; so immense
are they in their extent, so incessant in their exercise,
so terrible in their irreparable infamy. No doubt it
could never be foreseen, never be imagined, by those
who brought about and permitted the consolidation
of Italy into one kingdom, that the people, nominally
free, would become the abject slaves of a municipal
despotism and of a barbarous civic greed. None of
the enthusiasts for Italian independence possessed
that power of foresight which would have told them
that its issue would be the daily destruction, by
hordes of foreign workmen, of its treasures of art
and its landmarks of history. Yet there is no ex-

aggeration in saying that this, and nothing less than this, is its chief issue.

Hermann Grimm published a powerful appeal to the scholars and artists of Europe against the Italian destruction of Rome. Having for thirty years written on Italian cities and their art and history, with scholarship and devotion, he had gained the right to raise his voice in indignant protest and scorn against the mercenary and vulgar shamelessness with which the Roman municipality is so dealing with the splendid heritage which it has received, that soon scarcely one stone will be left upon another of the sacred city. He said, and with truth, that the portion of the Italian nation which has the eyes to perceive and the soul to abhor all that is being done is so small a minority, and one so spiritless, hopeless and discouraged, that it is for all practical purposes non-existent. He appealed to what he termed that larger Rome which exists in the hearts of all who have ever known Rome with a scholar's knowledge, or an artist's love. The appeal may be powerless but at least it may be heard ; and though it will scarcely be able to pierce through the thick hide of smug vanity and rapacity in which Italian municipalities are enveloped, it will put on record the courage and the scorn of one man for what is the greatest artistic iniquity of our time. It is idle and untrue for Italians to say that the rest of Europe has no right to interfere with what they do with the legacy they enjoy. In the first place, without the aid and acquiescence of Europe, the Italian kingdom as a unity could never have existed at all; without the permission of Europe the entry into Rome could never have been made at all. Europe has the title to observe and to condemn the manner in which the superb gift, which she permitted to be given to those very various peoples who are called Italians, is being squandered away and destroyed. The United Kingdom of Italy may, as a political fact, disappear to-morrow in any European war or any great Socialistic uprising; but historic Italy, classic Italy, artistic Italy, is a treasure which belongs to the whole world of culture, in which, indeed, the foreigner, if he be reverent of her soil, is far more truly her son than those born of her blood who violate her and desecrate her altars. Italy cannot be narrowed to the petty bounds of a kingdom created yesterday; she has been the mistress of all art, the muse and the priestess of all peoples.

What are the Italians doing with her? It is sickening to note and to record. Nothing can ever give back to the world what, day by day, municipal councillors having houses to sell, syndicates and companies merely looking for spoliation and speculation, contractors who seize on the land as a trooper seizes on a girl in a sacked town, are all taking from the fairest and the most ancient cities and towns on earth. The sound of the hatchet in the woods and gardens of Italy is incessantly echoed by the sound of the pickaxe and hammer in the cities and towns. The crash of falling trees is answered by the crash of falling marbles. All over the land, destruction, of the vilest and most vulgar kind, is at work; destruction before which the more excusable and more virile destruction of war looks almost noble. For the present destruction has no other motive, object, or mainspring than the lowest greed. It is absolutely

incomprehensible how, after having been the leaders
and the light of the far centuries, the Italians have,
by common consent and with pitiable self-congratula-
tion, sunk to the position of the most benighted
barbarism in art. In everything which is now constructed the worst and most offensive taste is manifest,
whilst that which has existed for centuries is attacked
and pulled down without remorse. I wholly fail to
account, on any philosophic or psychological grounds,
for the utter deadness of soul which has come on the
Italians as a nation. Born with loveliness of all kinds,
natural and architectural, around them, the æsthetic
sense should be as instinctive in them as their move-
ments of limbs or lungs. Instead of this, it is entirely
gone out of them. They have no feeling for colour, no
sense of symmetry, and little or no sense of reverence
for the greatness and the gloriousness of the past.

The only people in whom any of the native feeling
for natural and artistic beauty still exists are those
country people who dwell far removed from the
contagion of the towns, and the marine populations of
the Veneto. But even in these it is slighter than any
student of the past would expect. The sense of
colour is *nil* in most Italians ; they might as well be
colour-blind for any heed they take of harmony of
tones. They delight in *chinoiseries*, in photographs,
in crétonnes, in all the rubbish bought in modern
Exhibitions. In the superb and immense halls of a
palace of the Renaissance one will see priceless
tapestries on the walls, antique marbles on the
consoles, frescoes of Veronese, of Giulio Romano, or
of Sodoma on the ceilings ; and at the same time see
arm-chairs and couches, some yellow, some blue, some

green, some scarlet; a table-cover of crimson; and the mosaic floor covered with a worthless *moquette* carpet of all hues, and of a set and staring pattern. I call to mind a similar palace on the Tiber, whose very name is as a trumpet-call to all the glories of the past; there the antique statues have been coloured, 'because white marble is so cold and sad;' an admirable copy in bronze of the Mercury of Gian' di Bologna has had his wings, his petasus, and his caduceus gilded; and the marble floors have been taken up to have French parquet flooring laid down in their stead, and varnished so highly that the woods glisten like looking-glasses; yet the owner of and dweller in this place is a great noble, who, after his own fashion, cherishes art. I have seen a Greek Venus, found in the soil at Baiæ, wreathed round with innumerable yards of rose-coloured gauze by its owner, an Italian princess. The excuse given is, '*Senza un'po' di tinta sta cosi fredda!*'

It is the same feeling which makes the Italian peasant say of the field-flowers which you have arranged in your rooms, 'How well you have made those vulgar weeds look! Any one would take them now for *fiori secchi!*' (artificial flowers). Whence comes it, this absolute blindness of the eyes, this deadening absence of all consciousness of beauty? It is the same thing in their villages and their fairs. Go to a fair on a feast-day in any part of France; go to a kermesse in Belgium or Luxembourg; go to a merry-making in Germany or Austria, and you will see a picturesque and graceful sight; you will see a great deal of what the eyes of Teniers, of Ostade, of Callot, of Mieris saw in their day. There will be harmonised colours, unconscious grace of grouping, arrangements of common goods and simple things so made that beauty is got out of them. But in a village festival in Italy there is nothing, except in the water pageants of Venice, which is not ugly; it is all dusty, uninteresting, untempting; what colours there are, are arranged with the same disregard of fitness as is shown in the yellow, red and green arm-chairs of the palace chambers; and the whole effect is one of squalor and of vulgarity. The carnivals, which used to be fine and brilliant spectacles, are now, almost all, save that of Milan, mere tawdry, trivial, unlovely follies. Who can account for this?

Are we to infer that all the transmitted influences of race count for nothing? Would those who, rightly or wrongly, are tempted to explain all the problems of life by the doctrines of heredity tell me why the living representatives of the most artistic races on earth are almost absolutely deprived of all artistic instincts? Some have suggested that it is the outcome of the artificial habits and false taste of the eighteenth century; but this can scarcely be correct, because this artificiality existed all over Europe, not in Italy alone, and besides, never touched the country people in any way or in any of their habits.

The excuse made for the utter disregard and destruction of beauty in Italy is that the utility of all things is now preferred to beauty. But this is no adequate explanation. It may explain why a dirty steamboat is allowed to grind against the water-steps of the Ca'd'Oro, or why the fair shores of Poselippo and the blue bays of Spezzia and Taranto are made hideous by steam and bricks. But it will not explain why the peasant thinks a wax or cambric flower more lovely than a field anemone or daffodil, or why the nobleman paints his Athene and gilds the wings of his Hermes. This can only be traced to the utter decay of all feeling for beauty, natural or artistic, in the Italian mind, and, though we see, we cannot adequately explain, we can only deplore, it. There is no doubt a tendency all the world over to loss of the true sense of beauty ; despite the æsthetic pretences of nations, the real feeling for natural and artistic perfection is very weak in most of them. If it were strong and pure, the utilitarian (*i.e.*, the money-getting spirit) would not prevail as it does in architecture, and forest solitudes would not be destroyed as they are ; and men would see what hypocrites they be who make millions out of some hideous desecration of nature by factories, iron foundries, or petroleum wells, and think they can purchase condonation, and a reputation for fine taste, by buying pictures for their galleries or inlaying their halls with rare woods or stones. The whole world which calls itself civilised is guilty more or less of the most absolute barbarism ; but modern Italy is guiltiest of all, even as he who has inherited a fair home and cultured intelligence is guiltier than he who has never known anything but a vitiated atmosphere and a squalid house. It is the immensity of her heritage which makes her abuse of all her opportunities so glaring and so utterly beyond pardon.

Nothing can ever give back to mankind what every day the Italian municipalities and people are destroying, as indifferently as though they were pulling down dead leaves or kicking aside anthills in the sand.

There is not even the pretext for these acts that they are done to better the state of the people; to execute them the cheapest foreign labour is called in, ousting the men of the soil off it: house-rent is trebled and quadrupled, house-room narrowed, and in many instances denied, to the native population: and contracts are given away right and left to any foreign companies or syndicates who choose to bid for them. The frightful blocks of new houses, the hideous new streets, the filthy tramways, the naked new squares, are all made by foreign speculators who purchase the right of spoliation from the municipalities as the private owners of the soil. A few men are made temporarily richer: the country is permanently beggared.

'Rome,' wrote Hermann Grimm, 'represents for humanity a spiritual value which cannot be easily estimated, but which is none the less precious because ideal.' Yet the vulgar and petty administration of an ephemeral moment is allowed to treat the capital of the world as though it were some settlement of shanties in the backwoods of America, fit only to disappear beneath the mallet and scaffolding of carpenters and masons. He said with justice that to call it vandalism is an injustice to the Vandals, for they, at least, were too ignorant to know the worth of what they destroyed, and acted in mere fierce instinct of conquest, with no ulterior greed; but they who are now destroying arch on arch, tower on tower, temple and church and palace, piling the sacred stones one on another like rubble, and effacing landmarks which had been respected through a thousand years, have the excuse neither of ignorance nor of war. They know not what to do, and we may add that they care not what they do, so long as their gain is made, their pockets filled.

Of all the grotesque barbarisms committed in Rome, the destruction of the cloister of Ara Cœli and of the tower of San Paolo upon the Capitol, to make room for an equestrian statue of Victor Emmanuel, has been one of the most offensive and ill-judged. All the world knows the beauty of the Capitol, the immemorial memories connected with it, and the great statue which for so many centuries has felt the Roman sunshine strike on its golden bronze. The placing of a modern statue in juxtaposition with the mighty Aurelian is an act so irredeemably vulgar, so pitiably incongruous, that it is a matter of infinite regret, even for the repute of the House of Savoy, that the present king did not peremptorily forbid such use of his father's manes. In the Superga, or on the mountain-side of the Piedmontese Alps he loved so well, a statue of Victor Emmanuel would be in keeping with his traditions, but it is a cruelty to him to dwarf him by such surroundings and such memories as are there on the Capitol of Rome. His fame is not of the kind which can bear, uninjured, such comparisons; and were it even ten times greater than it is, there could be no excuse for using the Capitol for such a purpose when there is the whole width of the Campagna for it, and when, in perfect accord with the abilities of modern sculptors, there are all the staring and naked modern piazzas waiting for their works. Will it be credited that it was actually proposed to place a statue of him between the columns of St Mark? In these matters the king could and should, with perfect propriety, intervene, and forbid a pretended homage for his father's memory being made a pretext and cover for the coarse and common vandalism of the epoch. In Florence, the beautiful wooded entrance of the Cascine was destroyed to make the bald, uninteresting square called the Piazza degli Zuavi, and a large, stony, open place, shadeless and unlovely, was reserved for a monument to Victor Emmanuel; for this the oval brick basement of the pedestal was raised many years ago, and there stands, unfinished and hideous, an eyesore to the city, an insult to the royal House.

There is scarcely a little town, there is no provincial capital on the whole peninsula, which has not some new, staring, stucco street named Corso Vittorio Emmanuele, or some historic and ancient square made absurd and pitiable by being re-baptised Piazza dell' Independenza. The effect is at once ludicrous and deplorable.

If it were necessary thus to deify the events of the last thirty years, and magnify them out of their true proportions, it would have been easy to build some wholly new city in some vacant spot, which might have borne any name or names deemed fitting, and thus have left in peace the great cities of the past, and not have made the present recall the fable of the frog and the bull.

Around Rome, as well as within it, the most luxuriant vegetation, a few years ago, alternated with the most sacred ruins: tombs and temples and triumphal arches were framed in the most abundant foliage; the banksia rose, the orange, the myrtle, the jessamine climbed and blossomed amidst the ruins of the palace of the Cæsars. In all these grand gardens, in these flowering fields, in these grass meadows, stretching between their marble colonnades, there was, as the German scholar says, an infinite calm, a loveliness and stillness in which the poet and the scholar could draw near to the mighty dead who had once been there as living men. There was nothing like it left on earth. Now it is destroyed for ever. Now,—in the stead of that tender silence of the tombs, that exquisite freshness of the spring, awakening in a thousand moss-grown dells and myrtle thickets which had seen Ovid and St Paul, Augustine and Raffael—now, in the stead of this there are the stench of engines, the dust of shattered bricks, the scream of steam whistles, the mounds of rubbish, the poles of scaffolding, long lines of houses raised in frantic haste on malarious soil, enormous barracks, representative of the martial law required to hold in check a liberated people : all is dirt, noise, confusion, hideousness, crowding, clamour, avarice.

The leaders of an invading and victorious army would have been ashamed to cause the havoc and the blasphemy which the Roman municipality have carried out with shameless callousness ; the indignant voice of Europe would have bidden a Suwarrow, a Napoleon, a Constable de Bourbon stay his hand, had he dared to level with the dust the august monuments of which neither the majesty nor the memories have power to daunt the impious hand of the nineteenth century Edilizia. Common faith, even, has not been kept with the Roman people in the ruin of their city ; the completed plan, put before the public in 1880, of the works which were intended, did not prepare the public for one-tenth of the devastation which has been wrought. In the words of Grimm, those who put forth the plan of '80 proposed tranquil, moderate and decent measures, and never contemplated the insensate haste, the brutal fury, the unsparing greed shown by those who, professing to accept its propositions, have utterly disregarded and far outstripped them. In the plan of '80 it was, for instance, expressly stated and provided that certain gardens, amongst them the Ludovisi, should be purchased by the city, but kept intact in their verdure and extent. This promise has been broken.

What traveller has not known the Ludovisi Gardens? What scholar, dreamer, painter, has not found his heaven there? Those immemorial pines, making twilight beneath them in the sunniest noon, those lofty walls of bays and of arbutus, those dim, green, shadowy aisles leading to velvet swards and violet-studded banks, the family of peacocks spreading their purples, their emeralds, their gold, out in the glory of the radiant light, the nightingales singing night and day in the fragrant solitudes, Sappho's angel in Corrinna's gardens—who has not known these? who has not loved these? And they are gone, gone forever; gone through the greed of men, and in their stead will stand the vile rows of cheap and staring houses : in their place will reign the devil of centralisation.

Centralisation is the heart-disease of nations. The blood, driven by it from the body and the limbs, becomes turgid and congested, overfills the vessels of the heart, and chokes them up; there is no more health, and later there is death. It has been the

curse of France. It will be the curse of Italy.
The violated nymphs and the slaughtered nightingales
of the ruined gardens will be avenged.   But what
solace is that to us ? We have lost them forever.
No power on earth can give them back to us.

There is a violation of that sentiment which the
Latins called Piety, so glaring, and so monstrous, in
the destruction of Rome by the Italians, that it dwarfs
all similar ruin being wrought elsewhere.   All over
Italy things are daily being done which might wring
tears from the statues' eyes of stone.*

After the .outrage to Rome, the injury done to
Venice is the most irreparable, the most inexcusable.

The wanton destruction of the island of Saint
Elena is, after the destruction of the Ludovisi and
other historic gardens in Rome, the most disgraceful
act of the sacrilege of modern Italy.   It is barbarism
without one shadow of excuse or plea of obligation.
This loveliest isle had been spared by all hostile fleets
and armies.   It lies at the very mouth of the lagoon
opening out from the Grand Canal.   It arrests the
eyes of all who go to and fro the Lido.   It was, a
little while ago, a little paradise of solitude, fragrance
and beauty.   Its thickets of wild rose, of jessamine,
and of myrtle, were filled with song-birds.   Its old
church, the oldest in the Veneto, stood, grey and
venerable, amidst the shade of green acacias and
flowering oleanders.   The little world of blossom
and of melody, hung between the sea and sky, had a
holiness, a pathos, a perfection of woodland loveliness
not to be told in words ; there no sound was heard

* A Zoological Menagérie has been placed in the park of the
Villa Borghese !

except the bells of the matins and vespers, the lapping of the waves, the whir of the white gulls' wings, and the echo of some gondolier's boating song. To sit in its quiet cloisters, with the fragrance of its wild gardens all around, and see the sun set beyond Venice, and the deep rose of evening spread over the arch of the skies and the silver plain of the waters, was to live a little while in the same world that Giorgione and Veronese knew. It seems like a vision of a nightmare to find these cloisters levelled and these gardens and trees destroyed ; the whole island made a grimy, smoking mound of clay and ruins. Yet thus it is. The government has chosen to make it a site for a factory and foundry ; and, not content with this defilement, is throwing up, upon it and beside it, acres of the stinking sand and clay dredged up from the canals, intending in due time to cover this new soil with other factories and foundries, full in the face of the Ducal Palace, a few furlongs from the Piazza of St Mark. Viler devastation was never more iniquitously or more unpardonably wrought.

Meantime the very commonest care is refused to such interesting and priceless houses as the House of the Camel, which is let out to a number of poor and dirty tenants, with its eponymus alto-relievo made the target for the stones of the children ; while in the same quarter of the Madonna dell' Orta, close at hand, a manufacturer is allowed to send the mouths of his steam-tubes hissing through the iron arabesques and between the carved foliage of a most noble Gothic doorway belonging to a deserted church.

I am aware that it is useless to protest against these things. The soul in the country is withered up by small greeds. All these irreparable injuries are done that municipal councillors may pocket some gain, and any stranger who has the money necessary can purchase from the Conscript Fathers of the hour the right to defile, to annex, to violate, to destroy the fairest and most sacred places in Italy. The goddess is given over to the ravishing of any boor who brings a money-bag.

The scholar, the poet, the archæologist are all abhorred in modern Italy; their protests are impatiently derided, their reverence is contemptuously ridiculed, their love of art, of nature, or of history, is regarded as a folly, ill-timed and inconvenient, lunatic and hysterical. But the new-comer who proposes a machine, a chimney, a monster hotel, a bubble company, or a tramway station, is welcomed with open arms; it is considered that he means ' progress,' *i.e.*, that he means a subsidy for some one, a general scramble for gold pieces.

Emile de Lavaleye has demonstrated, in his recent *Lettres d'Italie*, that these works in Venice, so fatal to the city, cannot ever result in any financial profit; that, with coal forty francs a ton, it is impossible they should ever bring any; that all industry of the kind is artificial and pernicious in Italy, and ends in impoverishing the many to enrich a few.

It is a wanton love of destruction which can alone lead a people who possess neither iron nor coal to make foundries and factories in Venice, the most lovely and luminous city of the sea. These works cannot be ever profitable at Venice, by reason of the immense cost of the transport there of the metals and combustibles necessary for their development. Yet in every direction their foul smoke is rising, and dimming that translucent air so dear to every painter from Carpaccio to Aïvarnovski. From the Zattere alone no less than fourteen factory chimneys are visible.

The Fondamenté Nuové was in the days of the Doges the *riva*, consecrated to the villas and pleasure-gardens of the Venetian nobles ; their palaces were only for winter habitation or ceremonious use, but the beautiful garden-houses facing Murano were their retreat for mirth, ease and recreation of all kinds, with nothing between them and the silvery lagoon except the clouds of foliage and of blossom which then covered these little isles. Nothing would have been easier than to make this shore now what it was then, and it would even have been undoubtedly profitable to have done so. Will it be credited that, instead, it has been selected as the especial site of gas-works and iron-works and all abominations of stench and smoke, whilst, instead of the laughing loveliness of flowering lawns leaning to touch the sea, there is a long and dreary brick embankment, on which you can walk if you choose, and recall, if you can, the 'tender grace of a day that is dead'?

'*La lumière de Venise*' has been the theme of all poets and the enchantment of all travellers for centuries ; that opal-hued, translucent, ethereal light has been the wonder of every wanderer who has found himself in the enchantment of its silvery radiance. '*On nage dans la lumière*,' is the just expression of Taine, to describe the exquisite effulgence of the light in Venice. Yet this wonder, this delight, this gift of Nature from sea and sky, the modern masters of the fate of Venice deliberately sacrifice, that a few greedy commercial adventurers may set up their chimneys on the shores consecrated to St Mark.

The Venetian populace have still in themselves a sense of colour and a passion for verdure ; in every little *calle* and at every *traghetto* an acacia grows and a vine climbs ; on the sails of the fishing and fruit boats there are painted figures, and in the garb of those who steer them there is still picturesque choice of form and hue. But in the Venetian municipality, as in every other Italian municipality, all taste is dead, all shame is dead with it ; and the only exist-ence, the only passion, left in their stead, are those of gain and of destruction. On the Giudecca hideous factories, which belch out the blackest of smoke close to the dome of the Church of the Redentore, have been allowed to pollute the atmosphere and disgrace the view ; and in every shed or outhouse where any-one has a fancy to stick up the iron tube of an engine, similar smoke passes forth, making day frightful and clouding the lagoon for miles.

Reverence, and that sense of fitness which always goes with reverence, are wholly lacking in the modern Italian mind. There is a kind of babyish self-admira-tion in its stead, which is the most sterile of all moral ground, and with which it is impossible to argue, because it is deaf and blind, inwrapped in its own vanity. In a few years' time, if the Italian kingdom last, it will insist on its history being re-written, and the debts that it owed to the French Emperor in '59 and to the German Emperor in '70 being struck out of its balance-sheet altogether. Nothing was more untrue, more bombastical, or more misleading than the favourite phrase, *Italia fara da se ;* but it is one of those untruths which have been caressed and repeated until they are accepted as facts ; and the injury done by this conceit to the present generation is very great.

Nature has done all for Italy ; it is a soil which is indeed blessed of the gods ; from its pure and radiant air to its wildflowers, which spring as though Aphrodite were still here 'to sow them with her odorous foot,' it is by Nature perfectly dowered and thrice blessed. In its roseate dawns, its crystal, clear moonlight, its golden afternoons, it has still the lovely light of an unworn world. Art joined hands with Nature, and gave her best and her richest treasures to Italy. It is, to any scholar, artist, poet, or reverent pilgrim to her shrines, a thing of intolerable odium, of unutterable sorrow, that the very people born of her soil should be thus ignorant of her exquisite beauty, thus mercenary, venal and unshamed in their prostitution of it.

Even amongst those who follow art as their calling, there is no sense of colour or of fitness. When the old houses of the Via degli Archibusieri were pulled down in Florence, to lay bare the colonnade beneath them, a committee of artists deliberated for three months as to the best method of dealing with this colonnade. The result of their deliberations was to cover the old stone with stucco and paint the stones brown, with white borders ! The effect is enhanced by upright lamp-posts, coloured brown, stuck in the middle of the way. The excuse given for the demolition of the houses was that the removal of them would widen a thoroughfare: as the lamp-posts are much more obstructive to drivers than the houses were, the correctness of the reasons given can be easily gauged. This is an example of all the rest. 'Are we to go in rags for sake of being picturesque?' said a syndic now ruling one of the chief cities of Italy, to a person who complained to him of the destruction of art and beauty now common throughout the peninsula. The reply is characteristic of that illogical stupidity and that absolute colour-blindness which are common to the modern Italian, or, let us say, the municipal Italian mind. They are insensible themselves to the horror of their work, just as they are unconscious why yellow, blue and green chairs on a red carpet offend a delicate taste. To whitewash frescoed walls; to make old monasteries look brand new; to scrub and peel and skin sculptured marbles; to daub over beautiful arches and columns and cloisters with tempera paintings, mechanically reproduced in one set pattern over and over again, over miles of stucco ; to outrage the past and vulgarise the present; to respect nothing; to set the glaring seal of a despotic and bourgeois administration over all which ages have made lovely and reverent—all this they think an admirable and hygienic work, while they let human excrement be strewn broadcast over the fields and emptied in the street at midday under broiling heat, and set the guards of their rivers to drive out with blows of the scabbard the poor children who would fain splash and bathe in them under canicular suns. The excuse of hygiene is only the parrot cry which covers the passion for iconoclasm and destruction. To make their own *interessi* while the moment lasts is the only desire at the heart of all these civic councillors and engineers, architects and contractors, house-owners and speculators. To petty personal purposes and selfish personal profits everything is sacrificed by the innumerable prefects, syndics, and town councillors, by whom Italy is regarded as the Turkish pashas regarded the Egyptian fellah.

Florence, again, might, with great ease, have been made one of the most beautiful cities of Europe: if there had been only moderate care and decent taste displayed in its administration, its natural and architectural charms were so great that it would have been a facile task to keep them unharmed. If its suburbs, indeed, of ugliness and squalor, could show good roads and shady avenues ; if its river banks, instead of brick walls, showed grass and trees ; if its filthy cab-stands were kept out of sight, and its city trees allowed to grow at the will of Nature, Florence would be lovely and twice as healthy as it is. But there is no attempt to preserve what is beautiful, or to make what is of necessity modern accord in any manner with the old ; whilst on trees there is waged a war which can only oblige one to conclude that those who are entrusted with the care of them have no eye except to the filling of their own wood-cellars. It is a very common thing to see an avenue of plane or lime trees with their heads cut off, whilst all the trees, whether in the public gardens or on the boulevards, are chopped and hacked out of all likeness to themselves, and of course dry up and perish long before their time.

Nothing can be more criminal that what is actually

now being proposed in the Florençe town council, *i.e.*, to raise a loan of eight millions, at four per cent., to destroy the entire old centre of the city.* I repeat, nothing more criminal, more wasteful, or more senseless could be done. Florence is very poor; a few years ago she was on the brink of bankruptcy; taxation is enormous throughout Tuscany; the poorest are taxed for the very bed they lie on; the amount which she has to pay to the government from the *dazio consume* (that is, the octroi duty at the gates, on all food and produce of every kind entering the town) is extravagant and intolerable. So cruelly are the simplest productions of the soil mulcted by taxation that every class suffers, whether producer or consumer. The annual interest payable on the new loan will add immensely to the burdens which the city bears; and for what purpose is such a loan to be contracted? For the purpose of pulling down the oldest and most historic parts of Florence, to create a naked wilderness which will be changed into one of those squares, dusty and hideous, with metal lamp-posts round it and stunted shrubs in the centre of it, which represent to the municipal Italian the *ne plus ultra* of loveliness and civilisation. The excuse given of hygienic reasons is a lie. All the uncleanly classes which dwelt in the Ghetto have been bundled off wholesale to the S. Frediano quarters, where they will continue to dwell with unchanged habits, a few score of yards removed from where they were before. The dirt of Italian cities is not due to the age or shape of the streets, it is due to the filthy personal habits of the people,

* Since this was written it has been done, entirely obliterating republican Florence, and creating a new enormous debt for the town.

which are the same in a wide and roomy farm-house
in the pine woods as in a garret of a town. They
love dirt ; water never touches their bodies all the year
round, and never touches even their faces or hands in
winter ; they like their vegetables raw, their wine
sour ; their pipes are eternally in their mouths, and
their clothes reek with every stench under heaven. It
is the habits of the people, not the formation of the
streets, which constitute the standing peril of pestil-
ence in Italy. They would make a new house as
filthy as an old one in a week. For what, then, is this
enormous, useless, and unpardonable addition to the
civil debt of Florence incurred ? Only to put money
in the pockets of a few speculators, and a few owners
of the soil, at the cost of destroying all that is most
interesting, valuable, and historical in the city.

Will it be credited by any readers of these words
that it is actually in contemplation to turn the old
piazza behind the Palazzo Strozzi into a range of
glass-galleries like those of Milan or of Brussels ? It
is incredible that a whole civil population can tranquilly
permit such outrage, and such grotesque outrage, to
be committed in its name.

It is indeed very much as though the owner of
Raffaeles and Titians tore them up into tatters and
bought chromo-lithographs and olegraphs to hang in
their places.

Oftentimes the populace itself is pained and mor-
tified to see its old heirlooms torn down and its old
associations destroyed, but the populace has no power;
the whole civic power is vested in the bureaucracy,
and civic electoral rights are wholly misunderstood
and practically unused by the masses of the people.

It is for the most part the smug and self-complacent *bourgeoisie* which rules, and which finds a curious delight in the contemplation of everything which can destroy the cities of the Renaissance, and the records of classic Latium, to replace them with some gimcrack and brand-new imitation of a third-rate modern French or Belgian town, glaring with plate-glass, gilding, dust, smoke, acres of stucco, and oceans of asphalt.

The modern Italian has not the faintest conception of the kind of religious reverence with which the English, the German, the American scholar visits the cities of Italy. Such an emotion seems to the son of the soil wholly inexplicable and grotesquely sentimental. If the Englishman praise a monster hotel or a torpedo-boat, or the German the march of a regiment, or the American the shafts of a factory, then, and then only, will the Italian regard the travellers with complacency. And what is done in the cities is repeated in the small towns, of which the municipalities think it grand and 'advanced' to imitate the innovations of larger ones, and where the house-owners and owners of the soil are just as greedy as their town councillors, and just as eager to sacrifice any classic beauty or mediæval memory for gain.

Could Dante come to life, no curse that he ever breathed upon his countrymen would be one-half so fierce and deep as that with which he would devote the Italian of the close of the nineteenth century to the vengeance of the offended gods. But Dante's self would say his curses to deaf ears, wadded close with the wool of vanity and greed.

Meanwhile the taxation of all these towns is so high

that tradespeople are ruined in them, as the country proprietors are ruined in hundreds and thousands by the imposts on land and all that land produces. Against blind cupidity the gods themselves are impotent.

THE
FAILURE OF CHRISTIANITY

VERY soon, as the history of the world counts
time, Christianity will have completed its two
thousand years of existence. In some shape or other
its doctrines dominate the civilised portions of
Europe and America and Australasia; and even
in Asia and in Africa its representatives and
its missionaries are busied in the endeavours to
diffuse them into the dark places of the earth.
Whether we accept it as what is called a revealed
or supernatural religion, or whether we more ration-
ally consider it an offspring of the older and similar
myths of Asia united to Judaism, the fact remains the
same of the immense area of its adoption by the human
race, and especially by the Aryan race. Islamism is
widespread, but has no continuous power of proselyt-
ism similar to Christianity; and Judaism, though in-
exorably potent on the Jewish tribes, whatever
country they inhabit, can claim little or no power of
attracting strangers within its fold; does not, indeed,
seek to attract any.

To live and spread as it has done, Christianity must

have some vital force within itself superior to those possessed by other creeds. It must be suited to the human race in some manner which the religion of Mohammed and that of Israel have alike missed. Indeed, the whole history of the acquisition of its dominion is very singular, and has probably been due to the socialistic element contained in it ; for the gospels are a breviary intimately dear to the heart of every communist. Mohammedanism is aristocratic ; so is Judaism, so were the Greek and Latin religions ; but Christianity is the religion of democracy, of universal equality, of the poor man consoled for privation on earth by his belief that such privation is surely the narrow gate by which heaven alone can be reached. Even in the moment when Christianity most nearly approached an aristocratic worship, it still contained the germs of democracy ; it still held out hope to the poor man, hope both spiritual and material ; in the feudal ages, when it was the war-cry of knights and ruling power of great kings and arrogant priests, it still whispered in the ear of the swineherd and the scullion,—' Take my tonsure and my habit, and who knows that thou mayest not live to earn the triple crown ? '

Because Socialism is for a great part atheistic, it has been wholly forgotten how socialistic have been the influences on society of Christianity. The evangels are essentially the dream of a poor man ; the vision of a peasant asleep after a day of toil, and seeing in his vision the angels come for him, whilst they spurn the rich man on whose fields he has laboured. ' Come to Me, all ye who sorrow and are heavy-laden, and I will give you rest.' It is the invitation to the poor ;

not to the rich. The disciples are fishermen for the most part ; Christ ·is himself a carpenter ; the whole dream is a passion-play of peasants as entirely as that which represented it last year in Ammergau; and in it power, intellect and law are all subverted and proved wrong when Pilate gets down from the judgment-seat, and the watching fishers believe that they behold the resurrection.   This socialistic influence the doctrines of Christianity have had, and have gradually made felt throughout many ages, and are making felt more sharply and rudely in this our own than in any other age.   The most 'pious' of all sects are also always the most democratic ; the Nonconformists and the Wesleyans are always the most intent on levelling the barriers and irregularities of social life. Protestantism was the democratic daughter of the Papacy, but the Papacy was also a democrat when it made it possible for a swineherd to hold the keys of St Peter, and for a Becket to rule a Plantagenet, for a Wolsey to rule a Tudor.

Again and again the humble vassal lived to thunder excommunication upon monarchs, and the timid scribe who dared not lift his eyes from his scroll became the most powerful, the most arrogant, the most inexorable of churchmen.   It was this hope contained within it for the lowliest, this palm held out by it to the poorest, which made the enormous influence of Christianity from the days of Basil and Augustine to the days of Richelieu and Wolsey.   The feudal lords who shouted Christian war-cries, and the despotic kings who swore by the Holy Rood and by Our Lady, were wholly unconscious that in the creed they cherished there were the germs of the democratic influences which would in time to come undermine thrones and make aristocracy an empty name; they did not know that in Clement Marot's psalm-books and in Wycliffe's Bible there lay folded that which would in time to come bring forth the thesis of Bakounine and the demands of the Knights of Labour.

If we meditate on and realise the essentially socialistic tendencies of the Christian creed, we may wonder that the '*grands de la terre*' ever so welcomed it, or ever failed to see in it the death-germs of their own order ; but we shall completely understand why it fascinated all the labouring classes of mankind and planted in them those seeds of communism which are now bearing forth full fruit.   But what is almost equally certain is that Christianity will be wholly powerless to restrain the results of what it has inspired.

For of all absolutely powerless things on earth Christianity is the most powerless, even though sovereigns are still consecrated, multitudes still baptised, parliaments and tribunals still opened, and countless churches and cathedrals still built in its name.   It has become a shibboleth, a husk, a robe with no heart beating within it, a winged angel carved in dead wood.   It has said that it is almost impossible for the rich man to be just or inherit the kingdom of heaven: the Anarchists insist that it is utterly impossible, and will, if they can, cast the rich man into hell on earth.

Christianity has opened the flood-gates to Socialism ; but it will not have any power in itself to close them again.   For nothing can be in more complete contradiction than the prevalence of the profession of

Christianity with the impotency of that profession to colour and control human life. The Buddha of Galilee has not one-thousandth part of the direct influence on his professional disciples that is possessed by the Buddha of India. Christianity is professed over the whole earth wherever the Aryan race exists and rules, but all the kingdoms and republics which make it their state creed are, practically, wholly unaffected by its doctrines, except in so far as their socialistic members derive precedent and strength from them.

Take, for instance, that which governs states and prescribes the duties of men—the majesty of the law, as it is termed—the science and the practice of legislation. Side by side with the religion enjoined by the state there exists a code of legislation which violates every precept of Christianity, and resembles only the *lex talionis* of the old Hebrew law, which the Christian creed was supposed to have destroyed and superseded.

A savage insistence on having an eye for an eye and a tooth for a tooth is the foundation of all modern law. The European, or the American, or the Australasian, goes on Sunday to his church and says his formula, 'Forgive us our trespasses as we forgive those who trespass against us,' and then on the Monday morning prosecutes a boy who stole a ball of string, or a neighbour who has invaded a right of way, or an enemy whose cow has strayed, or whose horse has kicked, or whose dog has bitten, and exacts for one and all of these offences the uttermost penalty that the law will permit him to demand. It may be said that such law is absolutely necessary in civilised states : it may be so : but then the empty formula of the Christian forgiveness of trespasses should be in honesty abandoned.

Mr Ruskin never writes on Venice without dwelling on the vital influence of the Christian creed on the men of the middle ages, and contrasting the religious spirit of those whose cry was St Mark, and whose admiration was St Jerome, with those of modern times, when these names mean nothing on the ears of men. But, in truth, the influence was architectural and artistic rather than moral ; the memory neither of St Mark nor St Jerome ever prevented the blinding of the eyes of doges who had displeased the people, the treachery and brutality of their inexorable decrees, the torture of the Foscari, the betrayal of Carracciolo, the sale of slaves, or any one of the awful cruelties and tyrannies of the Council of Ten.

As it was in the Venice of the middle ages, so has it been and is wherever Christianity is nominally dominant. The cross is embroidered on banners and its psalter is carried to churches in pious hands, but its real influence on the life of nations is as slight as that of Mark and Jerome on the Council of Ten. The whole practical life of nations lives, breathes and holds its place by creeds and necessities which are the complete antithesis of the Christian ; they are selfish in their policies, bloodthirsty in their wars, cunning in their diplomacy, avaricious in their commerce, unsparing in their hours of victory. They are so, and, alas ! they must be so, or they would be pushed out of their place amongst nations, and parcelled out, like Joseph's coat, amongst their foes.

The capitalist who makes millions by the manufacture of rifled cannon sees no inconsistency in murmuring in his seat at Catholic mass or Protestant service, 'Return good for evil,' 'If one cheek be smitten, turn the other,' and all the rest of the evangelical injunctions to peace and forbearance : were any to suggest to him the inconsistency of his conduct, such an one would speak to deaf ears ; that his whole life was a violation of the precepts he professed would be an unintelligible reproach to him : his soul would take refuge, smug and safe, in his formulas.   Yet who can deny that, if the commands of Christianity had in the least penetrated beneath the surface of human life, to make weapons of destruction would be viewed as a crime so frightful that none would dare attempt it ? Some writer has said that ' singing psalms never yet prevented a grocer from sanding his sugar.' This rough joke expresses in a grotesque form what may be said in all seriousness of the impotency of Christianity to affect modern national life.

Christianity is a formula : it is nothing more.   The nations in which daily services in its honour are said in thousands and tens of thousands of cathedrals and churches, sell opium to the Chinese, cheat and slay red Indians, slaughter with every brutality the peaceful natives of Tonquin and Anam, carry fire and sword into central Asia, kill Africans like ants on expeditions, and keep a whole populace in the grip of military service from the Spree to the Elbe, from the Zuider Zee to the Tiber, from the Seine to the Neva. Whether the nation be England, America, France, Russia, Italy, or Germany, the fact is the same ; with the gospels on its reading-desks and their shibboleth on its lips, every nation practically follows the lusts and passions of its human greeds for possession of territory and increase of treasure. Not one amongst them is better in this matter than another. Krupp guns, shrapnel shells, nitro-glycerine and submarine torpedoes are the practical issues of evangelicism and catholicism all over the civilised world. And the nations are so sublimely unconscious of their own hypocrisy that they have blessings on their warfare pronounced by their ecclesiastics, and implore the Lord of Hosts for his sympathy before sending out armoured cruisers.

This is inevitable, is the reply : in the present state of hostility between all nations, the first one to re-nounce the arts of war would be swallowed up by the others. So it would be, no doubt ; but if this be the chief fruit of Christianity, may not this religion justly be said to have failed conspicuously in impress-ing itself upon mankind ? It has impressed its formulas ; not its spirit. It has sewn a phylactery on the hem of humanity's robe : it has never touched the soul of humanity beneath the robe. It has pro-duced the iniquities of the Inquisition, the egotism and celibacy of the monasteries, the fury of religious wars, the ferocity of the Hussite, of the Catholic, of the Puritan, of the Spaniard, of the Irish Orangeman and of the Irish Papist ; it has divided families, alienated friends, lighted the torch of civil war, and borne the virgin and the greybeard to the burning pile, broken delicate limbs upon the wheel and wrung the souls and bodies of innocent creatures on the rack : all this it has done, and done in the name of God.

But of mercy, of pity, of forbearance, of true self-sacrifice, what has it ever taught the world ?

A while ago there was published an account of the manufacture of the deadliest sort of dynamite on the shores of Arran. Full in the front of the great sea, with all the majesty of a rock-bound and solitary shore around them, these hideous works raise their blaspheming face to Nature and pollute and profane her most solemn glories ; and there, on this coast of Arran, numbers of young girls work at the devilish thing in wooden huts, with every moment the ever-present risk of women and huts being blown into millions of atoms if so much as a shred of metal, or even a ray of too warm sunshine, strike on the foul, sickly, infernal compound which their fingers handle. A brief while since two girls were thus blown into the air, and were so instantaneously and utterly anni-hilated that not a particle of their bodies or of their clothing could be recognised ; and all the while the sea-gulls were circling, and the waves leaping, and the clouds sailing, and deep calling to deep, 'Lo! behold the devil and all his works.' And there is no devil there at all except man—man who makes money out of this fell thing which blasts the beauties of Nature, and scars the faces of the hills, and has made possible to civilisation a fashion of wholesale assassination so horrible, so craven, and so treacher-ous that the boldness of open murder seems almost virtue beside it.

The manufactory of nitro-glycerine on the Arran shore is the emblem of the world which calls itself Christian. No doubt the canny Scots who are enriched by it go to their kirk religiously, are elders of it, very likely, and if they saw a boy trundle a hoop, or a girl use a needle on the Sabbath day, would think they saw a crime, and would summon and chastise the sinners.   Pontius Pilate was afraid and ashamed when he had condemned an innocent man ; but the modern followers of Christ have neither fear nor shame when they pile up gold on gold in their bankers' cellars through the death which they have manufactured and sold, indifferent though it should strike down a thousand innocent men.

Even of death Christianity has made a terror which was unknown to the gay calmness of the Pagan and the stoical repose of the Indian.   Never has death been the cause of such craven timidity as in the Christian world, to which, if Christians believed any part of what they profess, it would be the harbinger of glad tidings, the welcome messenger of a more perfect life.   To visionaries like Catherine of Siena, it may have been so at times, but to the masses of men and women professing the Christian faith, death has been and is the King of Terrors, from whose approach they cower in an agony which Petronius Arbiter would have ridiculed, and Socrates and Seneca have scorned. The Greek and the Latin gave dignity to death, and awaited it with philosophy and peace ; but the Christian beholds in it innumerable fears like a child's terror of ghosts in darkness, and by the manner of the funeral rites with which he celebrates it contrives to make grotesque even that mute majesty which rests with the dead slave as much as with the dead emperor.

Christianity has been cruel in much to the human race.   It has quenched much of the sweet joy and gladness of life ; it has caused the natural passions

and affections of it to be held as sins ; by its teaching
that the body should be despised, it has brought on
all the unnamable filth which was made a virtue in
the monastic orders, and which in the Italian, the
Spanish, the Russian peoples, and the poor of all
nations is a cherished and indestructible habit.   In
its permission to man to render subject to him all
other living creatures of the earth, it continued the
cruelty of the barbarian and of the pagan, and en-
dowed these with what appeared a divine authority—
an authority which Science, despising Christianity,
has yet not been ashamed to borrow and to use.

Let us, also, endeavour to realise the unutterable tor-
ments endured by men and maidens in their efforts to
subdue the natural desires of their senses and their
affections to the unnatural celibacy of the cloister, and
we shall see that the tortures inflicted by Christianity
have been more cruel than the cruelties of death.
Christianity has ever been the enemy of human love ;
it has forever cursed and expelled and crucified the
one passion which sweetens and smiles on human life,
which makes the desert blossom as the rose, and which
glorifies the common things and common ways of
earth.   It made of this, the angel of life, a shape of
sin and darkness, and bade the woman whose lips
were warm with the first kisses of her lover believe
herself accursed and ashamed.   Even in the unions
which it reluctantly permitted, it degraded and
dwarfed the passion which it could not entirely ex-
clude, and permitted it coarsely to exist for the mere
necessity of procreation.   The words of the Christian
nuptial service expressly say so.   Love, the winged
god of the immortals, became, in the Christian creed,

a thrice-damned and earth-bound devil, to be exor-
cised and loathed. This has been the greatest injury
that Christianity has ever done to the human race.
Love, the one supreme, unceasing source of human
felicity, the one sole joy which lifts the whole mortal
existence into the empyrean, was by it degraded into
the mere mechanical action of reproduction. It cut
the wings of Eros. Man, believing that he must no
longer love his mistress, woman, believing that she
must no longer love her lover, loved themselves, and
from the cloisters and from the churches there arose
a bitter, joyless, narrow, apprehensive passion which
believed itself to be religion, but was in truth only a
form of concentrated egotism, the agonised desire to
be ' saved,' to ascend into the highest heaven, let who
else would wait without its doors or pine in hell.
The influence of this is still with the world, and will
long be with it ; and its echo is still loud in the sibilant
voices which hiss at the poet who sings and the poet
who glorifies love.

And herein we approach that spurious offspring of
Christianity which is called cant.

Other religions have not been without it. The
Mosaic law had the Pharisee, who for a pretence made
long prayers. The Greek and the Latin had those
who made oblations to the gods for mere show, and
augurs who served the sacred altars with their tongue
in their cheek. But from Christianity, alas! has
arisen and spread a systematic hypocrisy more general,
more complete, more vain, more victorious than any
other. The forms of the Christian religion facilitate
this. Whether in the Catholic form of it, which
cleanses the sinner in the confessional that he may

go forth and sin again freely, or in the Protestant form, which, so long as a man listens to sermons and kneels at sacraments, does not disturb him as to the tenor of his private life, the Christian religion says, practically, to all its professors: 'Wear my livery and assemble in my courts; I ask no more of you in return for the moral reputation which I will give to you.'

Its lip-service and its empty rites have made it the easiest of all tasks for the usurer to cloak his cruelties, the miser to hide his avarice, the lawyer to condone his lies, the sinner of all social sins to purchase the social immunity from them by outward deference to churches.

The Christian religion, outwardly and even in intention humble, does, without meaning it, teach man to regard himself as the most important of all created things. Man surveys the starry heavens and hears with his ears of the plurality of worlds; yet his religion bids him believe that his alone out of these innumerable spheres is the object of his master's love and sacrifice. To save his world—whose common multitudes can be no more in the scale of creation than the billions of insects that build up a coral-reef beneath the deep sea—he is told that God himself took human shape, underwent human birth, was fed with human food, and suffered human pains. It is intelligible that, believing this, the most arrogant self-conceit has puffed up the human crowd, and that with the most cruel indifference they have sacrificed to themselves all the countless suffering multitudes which they are taught to call 'the beasts which perish.' It is this selfishness and self-esteem which, fostered in

the human race by Christianity, have far outweighed
and overborne the humility which its doctrines in
part strove to inculcate and the mercy which they
advocated.

It is in vain that the human race is bidden to
believe that its Creator cares for the lilies of the field
and for the birds of the air: it is the human race
alone for which [its God has suffered and died, so it
believes, and this solitary selection, this immense
supremacy, make it semi-divine in its own sight. It
is the leaven of egotism begotten by the Christian
creed which has neutralised the purity and the influence of its teachings. Here and there saintly men
and women have been guided by it solely in the
ways of holiness and unselfishness; but the great
majority of mankind has drawn from it chiefly two
lessons—self-concentration and socialism. 'Rock of
ages, cleft for *me*,' sighs the Christian; and this 'immense Me' is, as Emerson has said of it, the centre of
the universe in the belief of the unconscious egotist.

Christians repeat like a parrot's recitative the phrase
that no sparrow falls uncounted by its Creator, and
they go to their crops and scatter poison, or load
fowling-pieces with small shot to destroy hundreds of
sparrows in a morning. If they believed that their
God saw the little birds of the air fall, would they
dare to do it? Of course they would not; but they
do not believe: it only suits them to use their formula,
and they are never prevented by it from strewing
bird-poison or setting bird-traps.

Behold their priests taking on themselves the vows
of poverty, of chastity, and of renunciation, and
whether they be the Catholic cardinal, stately, luxuri-

ous and arrogant, or whether they be the Protestant bishop, with his liveried servants, his dinner parties, and his church patronage, what can we see more widely removed in unlikeness from all the precepts of the creed which they profess to obey? What fiercer polemics ever rage than those which wrangle about the body of religion? What judge would not be thought a madman who should from the bench counsel the man who has received a blow to bear it in meekness and turn the other cheek? What missionary would be excused for leaving his wife and children chargeable on parish rates because he pointed to the injunction to leave all that he had and follow Christ?

What attempt on the part of any community to put the precepts of Christianity into practical observance would not cause them to be denounced to magistrates as communists, as anarchists, as moonstruck dreamers, as lunatics? There are sects in Russia which endeavour to do so, and the police hunt them down like wild animals. They are only logically trying to carry out the precepts of the gospels, but they are regarded therefore as dangerous lunatics. They can have no place in the conventional civilisation of the world. What judge who should tell the two litigants in any lawsuit concerning property that they were violating every religious duty in wrangling with each other about filthy lucre would not be deemed a fool, and worse? The French Republic, in tearing down from its courts of law and from its class-rooms the emblems of Christianity, has done a rough, but sincere and consistent, act, if one offensive to a great portion of the nation ; and it may be alleged that this act is more

logical than the acts of those nations who open their
tribunals with rites of reverence towards a creed with
which the whole legislature governing these tribunals
is in entire and militant contradiction. 'Religion is
one thing; law is another,' said a lawyer once to
whom this strange discrepancy was commented on;
but so long as law is founded on assumptions and
principles wholly in violence with those of religion,
how can such religion be called the religion of the
state? It is as absurd a discrepancy as that with
which the Italian nation, calling itself Catholic, drove
out thousands of Catholic monks and Catholic nuns
from their religious houses and seized their possessions
by the force of the secular arm. It is not here the
question whether the suppression of the male and
female monastic orders was or was not right or necessary; what is certain is that the state, enforcing this
suppression, can with no shadow of sense or of logic
continue to call itself a Catholic state; as it still does
continue to call itself in the person of its king and
in its public decrees.

How is it to be accounted for—this impotence of
Christianity to affect the policies, politics, legislation
and general life of the nations which think their salvation lies in the profession of its creed? How is it
that a religion avowedly making peace and long-
suffering of injury the corner-stone of its temple has
had as its principal outcome war, both the fanaticism
of religious war and the avarice of civil war; a legislation founded on the *lex talionis* and inexorable in its
adherence to that law; and a commerce which all the
world over is saturated with the base desire to over-
reach, outwit and outstrip all competitors?

It is chiefly due to the absolutely 'unworkable' character of its injunctions; and partly due to the Jewish laws entering so largely into the creeds of modern Christians : also it is due to the fact that even in the purer creeds of the evangelists there is so much of egotism. 'What shall it profit a man if he gain the whole world and lose his own soul?' 'His own'—that throughout is to be the chief thought of his existence and its constant end. The greatest of the Christian martyrs were but egotists when they were not matoïdes. Their fortitude and constancy were already rewarded, in their belief, by every sweetness of celestial joys and glories. It may be doubted whether they even felt the scourge, the torch, the iron, or the rods, so intensely in their exaltation was their nervous system strung up to ecstasy. What could the poor offer of earthly life seem worth to those who believed that by thus losing it they would enter at once and forever into the exquisite consciousness of a surpassing beatitude? An intense, though innocent, selfishness was at the root of all the martyrdoms of the early Christian Church. There was not one amongst them which approached for unselfishness the death of Antinous. And it is surely this egotism which is an integral part of the Christian creed, and which has been at once its strength and its weakness; its strength in giving it dominion over human nature, and its weakness in allying it with baser things. The alloy has made the gold more workable, but has destroyed its purity.

Meanwhile, although the majority of Christian nations profess the Christian faith more or less sincerely, and give it at least the homage of hypocrisy, all the intellectual life of the world is leaving its folds without concealment. There is in its stead either the hard and soulless materialism of the scientist, or the sad, vague pantheism and pessimism of the scholar and the poet. Neither will ever suffice for the mass of mankind in general. The purely imaginative and intellectual mind can be content to wait before the immense unexplained enigma of life; it accepts its mystery, and sees the marvel of it, in the changing cloud, the blossoming weed, the wistful eyes of the beasts of burden, as much as it sees it in humanity itself. To such a mind the calmness and sadness of patience, and the kind of universal divinity which it finds in nature, can suffice : and to it the complacent conceit of science over the discovery of a new poison, or a hitherto unsuspected action of the biliary duct in mammals, must seem as childish and as narrow as does the belief in the creeds of the Papist, the Evangelical, or the Baptist. This is the only mental attitude which is at once philosophic and spiritual ; but it must ever remain the privilege of the few ; it can never be the possession of the multitude. The multitude will be forever cast into the arms of science, or of faith, either of which will alike flatter it with the assurance that it is the chief glory of creation, before which all the rest of creation is bound to lie subject in bonds and pain.

It is this selfishness and self-admiration which have neutralised in man the good which he should have gained from the simple benevolence of the Sermon on the Mount. A religion which is founded on the desire of men to attain eternal felicity will be naturally, seductive to them, but the keynote of its motive power can never be a lofty one.   The jewelled streets of the New Jerusalem are not more luxuriously dreamed of than the houris of the Mohammedan paradise.   Each form of celestial recompense is anticipated as reward for devotion to a creed.   And as all loyalty, all loveliness, all virtue *pèchent par la base* when they are founded on the expectation of personal gain, so the Christian religion has contained the radical defect of inciting its followers to obedience and faithfulness by a bribe—a grand bribe truly—nothing less than eternal life ; such life as the soul of man cannot even conceive ; but still a bribe.   Therefore Christianity has been powerless to enforce its own ethics on the world in the essence of their spirit, and has been perforce contented with hearing it recite its formulas.

What will be its future ?   There is no prophet of vision keen enough to behold.   The intellect of mankind is every year forsaking it more utterly, and the ever-increasing luxury which is possible with riches, and the ever-increasing materialism of all kinds of life into which mechanical labour enters, are forces which every year drive the multitudes farther and farther from its primitive tenets.   In a small, and a poor, community Christianity may be a creed possible in its practical realisation, and consistent in its simplicity of existence ; but in the mad world of modern life, with its overwhelming wealth and its overwhelming poverty, with its horrible satiety and its horrible hunger, with its fiendish greed and its ghastly crimes, its endless lusts and its cruel bitterness of hatreds, Christianity can only be one of two things—either a nullity, as it is now in all national life, or a dynamic force allied with and ruling through socialism, and destroying all civilisation as it, at present, stands.

Which will it be? There is no prophet to say. But whichever it be, there will be that in its future which, if it remain dominant, will make the cry of the poet the sigh of Humanity :

' Thou hast triumphed Opale Gallilean,
And the world has grown grey with Thy breath ! '

THE PASSING OF PHILOMEL

WILL there ever be a world in which the voice of Sappho's bird will be no longer heard?
I fear it.

For thrice a thousand years, to our knowledge, that divine music, the sweetest of any music upon earth, has been eloquent in the woods and the gardens of every springtime, renewing its song as the earth her youth. The nightingale has ever been the poet's darling; is indeed poetry incarnated; love, vocal and spiritual, made manifest. Nothing surely can show the deadness, dulness, coarseness, coldness of the human multitude so plainly as their indifference to this exquisite creature. Do even people who call themselves cultured care for the nightingale? How do they care? They rise from their dinner-table and stroll out on to a terrace or down an avenue, and there in the moonlight listen for a few moments, and say 'How charming!' then return to their flirtations, their theatricals, their baccarat or their bézique within doors. Bulbul may sing all night amongst the roses and the white heads of the lilies; they will not go out again. They prefer the cushioned lounge, the electric light, the tumbler of iced drink, the playing cards, the spiced *double entendre*. Here and there a woman may sit at her open casement half the night, or a poet walk entranced through the leafy lanes till dawn, but these listeners are few and far between.

When Nature gave this gift to the world she might well have looked for some slight gratitude. But save when Sappho has listened, or Meleager, or Shakespeare, or Ford, or Musset, or Shelley, or Lytton, who has cared ? Not one.

. Possibly, if the nightingale had been born once in a century, rarity might have secured for it attention, protection, appreciation. But singing everywhere, as it has done, wherever the climate was fit for it, through so many hundreds and hundreds of years, it has been almost wholly neglected by the soulless and dull ears of man.

A slender, bright and agile bird, the nightingale is neither shy nor useless, as it is said that most poets and musicians are. It eats grubs, worms, lice, small insects of all kinds, and hunts amongst the decaying leaves and grass for many a garden pest, with active energy and industry, qualities too often lacking to the human artist. It builds a loose, roomy nest, often absolutely on the ground, and always placed with entire confidence in man's good faith. It is a very happy bird, and its song is the most ecstatic hymn of joy. I never can imagine how it came to be associated with sorrow and tragedy, and the ghastly story of Procne and Itys. For rapturous happiness there is nothing to be compared to the full love-song of the nightingale. All other music is harsh, cold,

dissonant, beside it. But, alas! the full perfection
of the song is not always heard. For it to sing its
fullest, its richest, its longest, it must have been in
peace and security, it must have been left untroubled
and unalarmed, it must have its little heart at rest in
its leafy home. Where the nightingale is harassed,
and affrighted, and disturbed, its song is quite different
to what it is when in happiness and tranquillity; where
it feels alarmed and insecure it never acquires its full
song, the note is shorter and weaker, and the magnificent, seemingly unending, trills are never heard, for
the bird sings as though it were afraid of being heard
and hunted—which, indeed, no doubt it is.

When entirely secure from any interference, year
after year in the same spot (for, if not interfered with,
it returns unerringly to the same haunts), many
families will come to the same place together, and
the males call and shout to each other in the most
joyous emulation day and night. Under these conditions alone does the marvellous music of the nightingale reach its full height and eloquence. No one
who has not heard the song under these conditions
can judge of it as it is in its perfection : the strength
of it, the rapture of it, the long-sustained, breathless
tremulo, the wondrous roulades and arpeggios, the
exquisite liquid sweetness, surpassing in beauty every
other sound on earth.

In one spot, dearer to me than any upon earth,
where the old stones once felt the tread of the
armoured guards and the cuirassed priests of the great
Countess Matilda, the nightingales have nested and
sung by dozens in the bay and arbutus of the under-
growth of the woods, and under the wild roses and

pomegranates fringing the meadows. On one nook of grass land alone I have seen seven close together at daybreak, hunting for their breakfasts amongst the dewy blades, in amicable rivalry. Here they have come with the wild winds of March ever since Matilda's reign, and for many ages before that, when all which is now the vale of Arno was forest and marsh. Here, because long protected and beloved, they sing in the most marvellous concert, challenging and answering each other in a riot of melody more exquisite than any orchestra created by man can produce ; the long ecstasy pouring through the ardours of full noonday, or across the silver radiance of the moon ; saluting the dawn with joyous *Io triomphe!* or praising the starry glories of the night with a rapturous *Salve Regina!*

The hawks sweep through the sun rays, the owls flash through the shadows, but the nightingales sing on, fearless and unharmed ; it is only man they dread, and man cannot hurt them here.

Naturalists state that the nightingale does not attain to the uttermost splendour of its voice until the eighth or ninth year of its life, and that the song-sters of that age give lessons to the younger ones. To the truth of this latter fact I can vouch from personal observation, but I doubt so many years being required to develop the song to perfection. I think its perfection is dependent, as I have said, on the peace and security which the singer enjoys ; on its familiarity with its nesting haunts, and on the sense of safety which it enjoys. This may be said, in a measure, of the song of all birds ; but it is especi-ally true of the nightingale, which is one of the most sensitive and highly organised of sentient beings, and one, moreover, with intense affections, devoted to its mate, its offspring and its chosen home.

It will be objected to me that nightingales sing in captivity. They do so; but the song of the caged nightingale is intolerable to the ear which is used to the song of the free bird in wood and field and garden. It is not the same song; it has changed its character: it sounds like one long agonised note of appeal, and this indeed we may be certain that it. is.

I confess that I hold many crimes which are punishable by the felon's dock less infamous than the caging of nightingales, or indeed the caging of any winged creatures. Migratory birds, caged, suffer yet more than any, because, in addition to the loss of liberty, they suffer from the repression of those natural instincts of flight at certain periods of the year, which denial must torture them to an extent quite immeasurable by us. The force of the migratory instinct may be imagined by the fact that it is intense and dominant enough to impel a creature so small, so timid, and so defenceless as a song-bird to incur the greatest perils, and wing its unprotected way across seas and continents, mountains and deserts, from Europe to Asia or Africa, in a flight which is certainly one of the most marvellous of the many marvels of Nature to which men are so dully and so vain-gloriously indifferent. The intensity of the impelling power may be gauged by the miracle of its results; and the bird in whom this instinct is repressed and denied must suffer incredible agonies of longing and vain effort, as from unfit climate and from unchanged food. No one, I am sure, can measure the torture endured by migratory birds from these causes when in captivity. Russian women of the world are very fond of taking back to Russia with them nightingales of Southern Europe, for which they pay a high price: these birds invariably die after a week or two in Russia, but the abominable practice continues unchecked. Nightingales are captured or killed indiscriminately with other birds in all the countries where they nest, and no one seems alive to the shameless barbarity of such a sacrifice.

With every year their chosen haunts are more and more invaded by the builder, the cultivator, the trapper, the netter. Nightingales will nest contentedly in gardens where they are unmolested, but their preference is for wild ground, or at least for leafy shrubberies and thickets : the dense hedges of clipped bay or arbutus common to Italy are much favoured by them. Therefore the nudity characteristic of high farming is fatal to them : to Philomel and her brood shadow and shelter are a necessity.

Where I dwell, much is still unaltered since the days of Horace and Virgil. The 'silvery circle' of the reaping-hook still flashes amongst the bending wheat. The oxen still slowly draw the wooden plough up and down the uneven fields. The osiers still turn to gold above the flag-filled streamlets ; the barefooted peasants run through the flower-filled grass ; the cherries and plums tumble uncounted amongst the daisies ; the soft, soundless wings of swallow and owl and kestrel fan the air, as they sweep down from the old red-brown tiles of the roofs where they make their homes ; the corn is threshed by flails in the old way on the broad stone courts ; the vine and ash and peach and maple grow together, graceful and careless ; the patient ass turns in the circular path of the stone olive-press; the huge, round-bellied jars, the amphoræ of old, stand beside the horse-block at the doors ; the pigeons flash above the bean-fields and feast as they will ; the great walnut trees throw their shade over the pumpkins and the maize ; men and women and children still work and laugh, and lounge at noon amongst the sheaves, thank the gods, much as they did when Theocritus ate honey by the fountain's brink. But how long will this be so ? How long will the Italy of Virgil and Horace be left to us ?

Under the brutality of chemical agriculture the whole face of the world is changing. The England of Gilbert White and Thomas Bewick is going as the England of the Tudors went before it; and the France of the Bourbons is being effaced like the France of the Valois. The old hedgerow timber is felled. The cowslip meadows are turned into great grazing grounds. The high flowering hedges are cut to the root, or often stubbed up entirely, and their place filled by galvanised wire fencing. The wild-flowers cannot blossom on the naked earth ; so disap-pear. The drained soil has no longer any place for the worts and the rushes and the fennels and the water spurges. Instead of the beautiful old lichen-grown orchard trees, bending to the ground under the weight of their golden or russet balls, there are rows of grafts two feet high, bearing ponderous, flavourless prize fruits, or monotonous espaliers grimly trimmed and trained, with shot bullfinches or poisoned black-birds lying along their ugly length.

The extreme greed which characterises agriculture

and horticulture, as it characterises all other pursuits in modern times, will inevitably cause the gradual extermination of all living things which it is considered possible may interfere with the maximum of profit.   In the guano-dressed, phosphate-dosed, chemically-treated fields and gardens of the future, with their vegetables and fruits ripened by electric light, and their colouring and flavouring obtained by the artificial aids of the laboratory, there will be no place for piping linnet, rose-throated robin, gay chaffinch, tiny tit, or blue warbler; and none amidst the frames, the acids, the manures, the machines, the hydraulic engines, for Philomel.   The object of the gardener and the farmer is to produce: the garden and the farm will soon be mere factories of produce, ugly and sordid, like all other factories.

The vast expanses of unbroken corn lands and grazing lands, to be seen in modern England, have no leafy nooks, as the fields of Herrick, of Wordsworth, of Tennyson's earlier time had for them.   In Italy and in France the acids, phosphates, sublimates, and other chemicals, poured over vineyards and farm lands drive away the nightingale, which used to nest so happily under the low-growing vine leaves, or amongst the endive and parsley.   'The lands are never left at peace,' said a peasant to me not long ago; and the peace of the birds is gone with that of the fields: the fates of both are intimately interwoven and mutually dependent.   Where the orchard and the vineyard are still what they were of old—green, fragrant, dusky, happy places, full of sweet scents and of sweet sounds—there the birds still are happy.   But in the new-fangled fields, acid-drenched, sulphur-powdered, sul-

phate-poisoned, stripped bare and jealously denuded
of all alien life, winged and wild animals, hunted and
harassed, can have no place. Scientific husbandry
has sacrificed the simple joys of rural life, and with
them the lives of the birds. 'What shall it profit
a man if he gain the whole world and lose his
own soul?' has been asked by the wisdom of old.
The song of the birds is the voice of the soul of
Nature, and men stifle it for sake of avarice and
greed.

Three or four years ago the village of San Do-
menico, on the highway to Fiesole, was a green nest
which in spring was filled with the music of nightingales; the fields, with the wild-rose hedges, were one
paradise of song in springtime and early summer.
The old villa, which stands with its big trees between
the little streams of Africa and Mensola, where Walter
Savage Landor lived and where he wished to be
allowed to die, was hidden away under its deep cedar
shadows, and the nightingales day and night sang
amongst its narcissi and its jonquils. An American
came, bought and ruined. He could let nothing
alone. He had no sentiment or perception. He
built a new glaring wing, spoiling all the symmetry of
the old tenement, daubed over with new stucco and
colour the beautiful old hues of the ancient walls, cut
down trees by the old shady gateway, and built a
porter's lodge after the manner beloved of Hamp-
stead and of Clapham. He considers himself a man
of taste; he is (I am ashamed to say) a scholar! It
would have been less affront to the memory of Landor,
and to the spirits haunting this poetic, historic,
legendary place, to have razed the house to the

ground, and have let the grass grow over it as over grave.

Higher up, but quite near, on the same hillside as the villa of Landor, there stood a stone house, old, solid, coloured with the beautiful greys and browns of age ; it had at one side a stone staircase leading up to a sculptured and painted shrine, before it were grass terraces with some bamboos, some roses, some laurels and beneath these a lower garden which joined the fields and blended with them.   It was quite perfect in its own simple, ancient way.   A year ago the dreadful hand of the improver seized on it, daubed it over with staring stucco, painted and varnished its woodwork, stuck vulgar green *persiennes* in its old casements, and, in a word, made it as nearly as possible resemble the pert, paltry, staring, gimcrack structure of a modern villa.   It is now a blot on the hillside, an eyesore to the wayfarer, an offence to the sight and to the landscape ; and the nightingales, which were so eloquent on its grass terraces, go to its rosebushes and bamboos no more.

Such treatment as this of secluded places scares away the little brown lover of the moon : where there are brought all the pother and dust of masons', carpenters' and painters' work, the voice of Philomel cannot be heard ; the sweet solitude of the rose thicket is invaded by uncouth din and vulgar uproar ; the cedar shadows lie no more unbroken on the untrodden sward ; the small scops owl flits no more at evening through the perfumed air, the big white owl can nest no more beneath the moss-grown tiles and timbers of the roof; all the soft, silent, shy creatures of fur and feather, which have been happy so long, are startled, terrified, driven away for ever, and the nightingale dare nest no more. It is impossible to measure the injury done to the half-wild, half-tame denizens of the woods and gardens by the mania for restoration and innovation which characterises the purchasers and the tenants of the present day.

One such ghastly renovation as this, which has vulgarised and ruined the Landor villa and its neighbour, causes an amount of havoc to the creatures of the brake and bush which can never be repaired. Once frightened and driven out, they never come back again. They are the youth of the world; and, like all youth, once gone, they are gone for ever.

The builder who desecrated these places, the people who live in them, do not perceive the abomination which they have wrought; and if they were called to account, would stare at their accuser, understanding nothing of their sin. Are there not an admirably grained and varnished hall door, and window shutters of the brightest pistachio green? What matter if Philomel nest no more under the cuckoopint and burdock? Is there not the scream of the tramway whistle? What matter if the Madonna's herb grow no longer on the old stone steps and the swallow build no more under the hanging eaves? Are there not the painted boards declaring, in letters a foot long, that the adjacent land is to be let or sold for building purposes?

By the increase of bricks and mortar, and the sterility and nudity which accompany scientific agriculture, the nightingale is everywhere being driven higher into the hills, where it may still hope to nest unmolested, but where the temperature is unsuited to it. Its breeding grounds become, with every season, fewer and more difficult to find. It is sociable, and would willingly be at home in the gardens even of cities ; but men will not leave it in peace there. Its nests are taken and its feeding grounds are destroyed by the over-sweeping and over-weeding of the modern gardener. The insensate modern practice of clearing away all leaves as they fall from the soil of shrubberies and avenues starves the nightingales, as it starves the roots of the trees. When the leaves are left to lie through the winter the trees rejoice in their warmth and nourishment, and the returning birds find a rich larder in the spring. A carpet of golden leaves is a lovely and useful thing ; but the modern gardener does not think so, and his intolerable birch broom, and yet more intolerable mechanical sweeper, tears away the precious veil which Nature's care would spread in preservation over the chilly earth.

Starved, hunted, robbed of its nest, and harassed in its song, the nightingale must therefore inevitably grow rarer and rarer every year.

The vile tramways, which have unrolled their hideous length over so many thousands of miles all over Europe, bring the noise, the glare, and the dirt of cities into the once peaceful solitude of hill and valley. They are at this moment being made through the beautiful forest roads of the Jura !

The curse of the town is being spread broadcast over the face of the country, as the filth of urban cesspools is being carried out over rustic fields. The sticks, the guns, the nets, the traps, the birdlime of the accursed bird destroyer, are carried by train and tram into the green heart of once tranquil wolds and

woods. The golden gorse serves to shelter the
grinning excursionist, the wild hyacinths are crushed
under the wine flasks and the beer bottles. The
lowest forms of human life leave the slums and
ravage the virgin country; ten thousand jarring
wheels carry twenty thousand clumsy, greedy hands
to tear down the wild honeysuckle and pull to pieces
the bird's nest, to tear up the meadow-sweet and
strangle the green lizard. The curse of the town
mounts higher and higher and higher every year, and
clings like a vampire to the country, and sucks out
of it all its beauty, and stifles in it all its song.

Soon the hiss of the engine and the bray of the
cad will be the only sounds heard throughout Europe.
It is very probable that the conditions of human life
in the future will be incompatible with the existence
of the nightingale at all. It is almost certain that
all natural beauty, all woodland solitude, all sylvan
quiet, will be year by year more and more attacked,
diminished, and disturbed, until the lives of all
creatures which depend on these will come altogether
to an end.

Let us imagine what the world was like when
Sappho heard the nightingales of Greece, and we can
then measure by our own present loss what will be
the probable loss of future generations; the atmosphere was then of a perfect purity; no coal smoke
soiled the air or blurred the sea; no engine hissed,
no cogwheel whirred, no piston throbbed; the sweet
wild country ran to the very gates of the small cities;
there was no tread noisier than the footfall of the
ox upon the turf; there was no artificial light harsher
than the pale soft gleam of the olive oil, the temples

were white as the snow on Ida, and the brooks and
the fountains were clear as the sparkling smile of
the undimmed day.   In such a world every tuft of
thyme and every bough of laurel had its nest,
and under the radiant skies the song of the nightingales must have been eloquent over all the plains
and hills in one unbroken flood of joy.

Let us picture the fairness of the world as it was
then, with undimmed skies, unpolluted waters, un-
touched forests, and untainted air; and we must
realise that what is called civilisation has given us
nothing worth that which it has taken, and will
continue to take away from us, forever.

THE ITALY OF TO-DAY

CAVALLOTTI * has written, in his letter of protest against the arrest of the Sicilian deputy, De Felice, a sentence which deserves to be repeated all over the land : one of those sentences, *multum in parvo*, which resume a whole situation in a phrase : he has written : 'Invece che del pane si da il piombo.' Instead of bread to the suffering and famished multitudes there is offered lead, the lead of rifle bullets and of cannon-balls. That is the only response which has as yet been given to demands which are in the main essentially just. Is the English public aware that the Italian city of Caltanissetta has been, the first week of the year, bombarded by Italian artillery, and that in that town alone six hundred arrests have been made in one day? If this were taking place in Poland the English public and its press would be convulsed with rage.

The attitude of the press in England towards the present Italian struggle against overwhelming fiscal burdens is so singular that it can only be attributed to one of two things : Bourse interests or German

* Deputy for Corteolona, and leader of the Extreme Left.

influence. All that is said in the English press concerning Italian affairs is at all times marked by singular ineptitude and inaccuracy; but at the present crisis it is conspicuous for a resolute and unblushing concealment of facts. The unfortunate flattery which has been poured out on Italy by the German press and Parliament for their emperor's ends, and by the English press and Parliament out of hatred of France, has been taken for gospel truth by the Quirinale, the Palazzo Braschi, and every deputy and editor from Alps to Etna, and has fed the natural vanity of the Italian disposition, until, in a rude awakening, the whole nation finds itself on the brink of bankruptcy and anarchy.

To all conversant with the true state and real needs of the country ever since the death of Victor Emmanuel, the language of the German and English press and Parliaments has seemed almost insane in its optimism, as it has been most cruel in its fulsome falsehood. Much of the present woe may be attributed to it; for if Berlin and London had not taken, or pretended to take, Messer Francesco Crispi for a statesman, it is very possible that that ingenious lawyer might never have dragged his sovereign into the meshes of the Triple Alliance and the Slough of Despond of a bottomless debt. That unintelligent and interested flattery is as injurious to nations as to individuals and gives them vertigo, is a truth too frequently forgotten or purposely disregarded.

Perhaps one of the oddest and least admirable traits in the public opinion of the latest half of this century is its absolute unconsciousness of its own caprices and inconsequence; its entire ignorance of

how flatly its assertions of to-day contradict those of
yesterday and will be contradicted by those of to-
morrow. History has accustomed us to such trans-
mogrifications, and we know that power is potent to
turn the insurgent into the reactionist, but certainly
the drollest and most picturesque episode in connec-
tion with the Sicilian revolution is the arrest of the
deputy De Felice, for inciting to civil war, coupled
with the fact that the last deputy arrested for precisely the same cause was Francesco Crispi at the
time of Aspromonte! History, in all its length and
breadth, does not furnish us with any droller antithesis
than that of Crispi as arrested and Crispi as arrester.
The Italian press has contented itself with merely
stating the circumstances, and letting them speak for
themselves ; the European press does not appear even
to be aware of them. For the European press, with
the exception of the French, the Crispi of Aspromonte
is dead and buried, as the Crispi of Montecitorio and
the Quirinale would desire that he should be. The
prostration of the English press in especial before
the latter is infinitely comical to those who know the
real career of the fortunate Sicilian notary who began
life as a penniless republican, and is ending it as a
plutocrat, a reactionist, and a Knight of the Order of
the Association. It is probable that Europe on the
whole knows but little of the Crispi of Aspromonte ;
it is possible that De Felice and his friends will cause
it to know more. Falstaff abjuring cakes and ale,
and putting two mirthful roysterers in the pillory,
would present the only companion picture worthy of
comparison with the Crispi of Montecitorio gravely
defending the seizure of the leader of the Fasci on the

score that the offence of the latter is *lesa alla patria*.
Why is revolutionary effort in '93 and '94 treason to
the country when revolutionary effort in '59 and '48
was, we are taught by all Italian text-books, the most
admirable patriotism? It is a plain question which
will never be honoured by an answer. Crispi of
Montecitorio does not condescend to reason; he finds
it easier to use cannon and bayonets, as they were
used against that Crispi of Aspromonte of whom he
considers it ill-bred in anyone to remind him. Crispi
understands the present era; he knows that it does
not punish, or even notice, such inconsistencies, at
least when they are the inconsistencies of successful
men.

Were the national sense of humour as quick as it
was in the days of Pulci and Boiardo this circumstance would be fatal to the dictatorship of the ex-
revolutionist.

In the national litany of Italy the chief of gods
invoked are Mazzini, Ugo Foscolo, Garibaldi, Manini,
and a score of others of the same persuasion, and all
the present generation (outside what are termed Black
Society and Codini Circles) are reared in religious
veneration of such names. Now, it does not matter
in the least whether this veneration be well or ill
founded, be wise or unwise; it has been taught to all
the present youth and manhood of all liberal-minded
Italian families as a duty, a pleasure, and a creed in
one. What sense is there in blaming this multitude
if they carry out their own principles to a logical conclusion, and refuse to see that the opinions which
were noble and heroic in their fathers become treason
and crime in themselves? The House of Savoy, by

a lucky chance for itself, drew the biggest prize in the lottery of national events in 1859; but it was not to place the House of Savoy on the Italian throne that Garibaldi fought, and Mazzini conspired, and a host of heroes died in battle or in exile. To all those whose names are like trumpet-calls to us still, the merging of their ideal of United Italy into a mere royal state must have seemed bathos, must have caused the most cruel and heartbreaking disillusion. They accepted it because at the time, rightly or wrongly, they considered that they could do no less; but they suffered, as all must suffer who have cherished high and pure dreams and behold what is called the realisation of them in the common clay of ordinary circumstance.

No one can pretend that the chief makers of the union of the country were monarchical. They were Red ; and were hunted, imprisoned, exiled, shot for the colour of their opinions, precisely in the same manner as the leaders of the Fasci and the deputies of the Extreme Left are being dealt with now. Measures of this kind are excusable in absolute or arbitrary governments, such as Russia or Prussia ; but in a State which owes its very existence to revolutionary forces, they are an anomaly. It is truly the sad and sorry spectacle of the son turning on and strangling the father who begat him.

At the present date Italy is a military tyranny. It is useless to deny the fact. Many parts of the country are in a state of siege, as though actually invaded and conquered ; and although recent events are alleged in excuse for this, it is by no means the first time that the army has been used for the suffocation of all public expression of feeling. Arbitrary

and unexplained arrest has always been frequent;
and when the sovereigns visit any city or town the
gaols thereof have always been filled on the vigil of
the visit with crowds of persons suspected of democratic or dangerous tendencies.   A rigid censorship
of telegrams has long existed, as inquisitorial as any
censorship of an *ancien régime;* and at the present
moment telegrams from Sicily are absolutely forbidden to be despatched.   Wholesale invasion of the
privacy of private houses takes place at the pleasure
of the police, and seizure of private letters and papers
follows at the caprice of the Questura.

Where is there any pretext of liberty?   In what
does the absolutism of 1894 differ from that of the
Bourbon, or of the Este-Lorraine?   In what sense can
a Free Italy be said to exist?   The Gallophobia now
so general amongst English political speakers and
writers may account for the determination in them
to applaud the Italian Government, alike when it is
wrong as when it is right; but it is quite certain that,
whatever be the motive, the English press has, with
very few exceptions, combined to hide from the
English public the true circumstances and causes of a
revolution which, however to be deplored in its ex-
cesses, is not a whit more blameable, or less interesting and excusable than the other revolutions of Italy
which filled England with such delight and sympathy.   The kingdom of Italy was created by revolution.   As the life of a nation counts, it was but yesterday that Garibaldi's red shirt was pushed through
the gates of Stafford House, narrowly escaping
being torn to rags by the admiring and enthusiastic
crowds of London.   To the philosophic observer

there is something extremely illogical in the present denunciation of men who are now doing nothing more than Garibaldi did with the applause of Europe and America. To set up statues in every public square to Garibaldi, and imprison Garibaldi Bosco, and charge with high treason De Felice Giuffrida, is a nonsense to which it is difficult to render homage.

It is well known that the King, unconstitutionally, refused to accept the Zanardelli Ministry because it would have led to reduction of the army, and, as a necessary consequence, to withdrawal from the German incubus. He is possessed with a mania for German influences ; influences, of all others, the most fatal to public freedom and political liberty. Nothing in the whole world could have been so injurious to Italy as to fall, as she has done, under the mailed hand of the brutal Prussian example and exactions.

Germany has always been fatal to Italy, and always will be. The costly armaments which have made her penniless are due to Germany. Her army and navy receive annual and insulting inspection by Prussian princes. The time will probably come when German troops will be asked to preserve 'social order' in the cities and provinces of Italy. So long as the German alliance continues in its present form, so long will this danger for Italy always exist, that, in the event of the Italian army proving insufficient, or unwilling, to quell revolution, the timidity or despotism of Italian rulers may beg the aid of Germany to do so.

In the manifesto of the Extreme Left, after the fall of Giolitti, the state of the country was described in language forcible but entirely true.

'Commerce is stagnant, bankruptcy general, savings are seized, small proprietors succumb under fiscal exactions, agriculture languishes, stifled under taxation, emigration is increased in an alarming proportion to the population, the municipalities squander and become penniless; the country, in taxes of various kinds, pays no less than seventy per cent., *i.e.*, four or five times as much as is paid by rich nations. The material taxable diminishes every day, because production is paralysed in its most vital parts, and misery has shrunken consumption; in a word, the whole land is devoured by military exactions and the criminal folly of a policy given over to interests and ambitions which totally ignore the true necessities of the people. The hour is come to cry, " Hold, enough!" and to oblige the State not to impose burdens, but to make atonement.'

There is nothing exaggerated in these statements; they are strictly moderate, and understate the truth. The Extreme Left may or may not be Socialistic, but in its manifesto it is entirely within the truth, and describes with moderation a state of national suffering and penury which would render pardonable the greatest violence of language.

The Extreme Left affirms with the strictest truth that its members have never contributed to bring about the present misery, and are in no degree responsible for it. The entire responsibility lies with corrupt administration, and with military tyranny and extravagance.

When a people are stripped bare, and reduced to destitution, can it be expected, should it be dreamed, that they can keep their souls in patience when fresh taxes threaten them, and the hideous Juggernauth of military expenditure rolls over their ruined lives?

Italians have been too long deluded with the fables of men in office ; and many years too long, patient under the intolerable exactions laid upon them. It is not only the imperial, but the municipal tyrannies which destroy them ; they are between the devil and the deep sea ; what the State does not take the Commune seizes. The most onerous and absurd fines await every trifling sin of omission or commission, every insignificant, unimportant, little forgetfulness leads to a penalty ridiculously disproportioned to the trifling offence—a little dust swept on to the pavement, a dog running loose, a cart left before a door, a guitar played in the street, a siesta taken under a colonnade, a lemon or a melon sold without permit to trade being previously purchased and registered, some infinitesimal trifle—for which the offender is dragged before the police and the municipal clerks, and mulcted in sums of three, five, ten, twenty, or thirty francs. Frequently a fine of two francs is quite enough to ruin the hapless offender. If he cannot pay he goes to prison.

The imperial tax of *ricchezza mobile* is levied on the poorest ; often the bed has to be sold or the saucepans pawned to pay it. The pawning institutes are State affairs ; their fee is nine per cent., and the goods are liable to be sold in a year. In France the fee is four per cent., and the goods are not liable to be sold for three years. When a poor person has scraped the money together to pay the fees, the official (*stimatore*) often declares that the article is more worthless than he thought, and claims a *calo* of from ten to a hundred francs, according to his caprice; if the *calo* be not paid the object is sold, though the nine per cent. for the past year may have been paid on it. The gate-tax, *dazio consumo*, best known to English ears as *octroi*, which has been the especial object of the Sicilian fury, is a curse to the whole land. Nothing can pass the gates of any city or town without paying this odious and inquisitorial impost. Strings of cattle and of carts wait outside from midnight to morning, the poor beasts lying down in the winter mud and summer dust. Half the life of the country people is consumed in this senseless stoppage and struggle at the gates; a poor old woman cannot take a few eggs her hen has laid, or a bit of spinning she has done, through the gates without paying for them. The wretched live chickens and ducks, geese and turkeys, wait half a day and a whole night cooped up in stifling crates or hung neck downwards in a bunch on a nail; the oxen and calves are kept without food three or four days before their passage through the gates, that they may weigh less when put in the scales. By this insensate method of taxation all the food taken into the cities and towns is deteriorated. The prating and interfering officers of hygiene do not attend to this, the greatest danger of all to health, *i.e.*, inflamed and injured carcasses of animals and poultry sent as food into the markets.

The municipalities exact the last centime from their prey; whole families are ruined and disappear through the exactions of their communes, who persist in squeezing what is already drained dry as a bone. The impious and insensate destruction of ancient quarters and noble edifices goes on because the municipal councillors, and engineers, and contractors fatten on it. The cost to the towns is enormous, the damage done is eternal, the debt incurred is incalculable, the loss to art and history immeasurable, but the officials who strut their little hour on the communal stage make their profits, and no one cares a straw how the city, town, or village suffer.

If the Italian States could have been united like the United States of America, and made strictly neutral like Belgium, their condition would have been much simpler, happier, and less costly. As a monarchy, vanity and display have ruined the country, while the one supreme advantage which she might have enjoyed, that of keeping herself free to remain the courted of all, she has wilfully and stupidly thrown away, by binding herself, hand and foot, almost in vassalage, to Prussia. For this, there can be no doubt, unfortunately, that the present King is mainly responsible; and, strange to say, he does not even seem to be sensible of the magnitude of the evil of his act.

It is as certain as any event which has not happened can be, that nothing of what has now come to pass would have occurred but for the disastrous folly which has made the Government of Italy strain to become what is called a Great Power, and conclude alliances of which the unalterable condition has been a standing army of as vast extent as the expenditure for its maintenance is enormous. There is nothing abnormal in the present ruin of the country, nothing which cannot easily be traced to its cause, nothing which could not have been avoided by prudence, by modesty, and by renunciation. As the pitiful vanity and ambition to reach a higher grade than that which is naturally theirs beggars private individuals, so the craze to be equal with the largest empire, and to make an equal military and naval display with theirs, has caused a drain on the resources of the country, a pitiless pressure upon the most powerless and hopeless classes, which have spread misery broadcast over the land.

It might be deplorable, unwise, possibly thankless, if the country dismissed the House of Savoy; but in so doing the country would be wholly within its rights. The act would be in no sense whatever *lesa alla patria;* it might, on the contrary, be decided on, and carried out, through the very truest patriotism. The error of the House of Savoy is the same error as that of the House of Bonaparte; they forget that what has been given by a plebiscite, a later plebiscite has every right and faculty to withdraw. The English nation, when it put William of Orange on the throne, would have been as entirely within its rights and privileges had it put him down from it. When a sovereign accepts a crown from the vote of a majority, he must in reason admit that another larger and later majority can withdraw it from his keeping. A plebiscite cannot confer Divine Right. It cannot either confer any inalienable right at all. It is, therefore, entirely illogical and unjust to visit the endeavour and desire to make Italy a republic as a crime of high treason. An Italian has as much right to wish for a republican form of government, and to do what he can to bring it about, as the Americans of the last century had to struggle against the taxation of George III. And if the Casa Savoia be driven from the Quirinale, it will owe this loss of power entirely to its own policy, which has impoverished the nation beyond all endurance. The present King's lamentable and inexplicable infatuation for the German alliance, and all the frightful expenditure and sacrifice to which this fatal alliance has led, have brought the country to its present ruin.

At the moment at which these lines are written, the flames of revolution are destroying the public buildings of the city of Bari; before even these lines can be printed, who shall say that these flames may not have spread to every town in the Peninsula? Of course, the present revolts may be crushed by sheer armed force; but if a reign of terror paralyse the movement for awhile, if a military despotism crush and gag the life out of Palermo and Naples and Rome, as it has been crushed and gagged by similar means in Warsaw and in Moscow, the causes which have led to revolution will continue to exist, and its fires will but die down awhile, to break forth in greater fury in a near future. The Crispi of Montecitorio is now busy throwing into prison all over the country a large number of citizens, for doing precisely the same things as the Crispi of Aspromonte did himself, or endeavoured to do. But in the present age a man may abjure and ignore his own past with impunity. As it is always perfectly useless to refute Mr Gladstone's statements by quotations from his own earlier utterances, so it would be quite useless to hope to embarrass the Italian premier by any reminder of his own younger and revolutionary self. Renegades

always are impervious to sarcasm, and pachyder-
matous against all reproach.

Crispi is very far from a great man in any sense of
those words, *Au pays des aveugles le borgne est roi*,
and he has had the supreme good fortune to have
outlived all Italian men of eminence. If Cavour and
Victor Emmanuel were living still, or even Sella and
Minghetti and La Marmora, it is extremely probable
that the costly amusement of making Crispi of
Aspromonte First Minister of the Crown would
never have been amongst the freaks of fate. He
has had 'staying power,' and so has buried all those
who would have kept him in his proper place. It is
possible that if he had adhered to his earlier creeds
he might have been by this time President of an
Italian Republic, for his intelligence is keen and
versatile, and his audacity is great and elastic. But
he has preferred the more prosperous and less glorious career of a minister and a *maire du palais*. He
has emerged with amazing insolence from financial
discredit which would have made any other man
ashamed to face the social and political worlds ; and,
mirabile dictu ! having dragged his King and country
into an abyss of poverty, shame and misery, he is still
adored by the one and suffered to domineer over the
other.

Successful in the vulgar sense of riches, of decora-
tions, of temporary power, and of overweening Court
favour, the Sicilian man of law is ; successful in the
higher sense of statesmanship, and the consolation of
a suffering nation, he never will be. And that he has
been permitted to return to power is painful proof of
the weakness of will and the moral degradation of

the country.   There is no great man in Italy at the present hour, no man with the magnetism of Garibaldi, or the intellect of D'Azeglio, or even the rough martial talent of Victor Emmanuel, and in the absence of such the sly, subtle, fox-like lawyers, by whom the country is overrun, come to the front, and add one curse more to the many curses already lying on the head of Leopardi's beloved Mater Dolorosa. It is possible that, for want of a man of genius who would be able to gather into one the scattered forces, and fuse them into irresistible might by that magic which genius alone possesses, the cause of liberty will be once more lost in Italy.   If such a leader do not appear, the present movement, which is not a revolt but a revolution in embryo, will probably be trampled out by armed despotism, and the present terror of the ruling classes of Europe before the bugbear of anarchy will be appealed to in justification of the refusal to a ruined people of the reforms and the atonement which they have, with full right, demanded.

January 1894.

BLIND GUIDES

A MONGST the famous gardens of the world, the Orti Oricellari* must take a foremost place, alike for sylvan beauty and for intellectual tradition. Second only to the marvellous gardens of Rome, they were first, for loveliness and for association, amongst the many great and carefully-cultured gardens which once adorned Tuscany. Under the Rucellai their superb groves and glades sheltered the most intellectual meetings which Florence has ever seen. The Società Oricellari (which continued that imitation of the Platonic Academy created by Cosimo and Lorenzo) assembled here under the shade of the great forest trees. Here Machiavelli read aloud his Art of War, and here Giovanni Rucellai composed his Rosamunda. The house built for Bernardo Rucellai by Leon Battista Alberti was a treasure-house of art, ancient and contemporary; and learning, literature and philosophy found their meet home under the ilex and cedar shadows, and in the fragrant air of the orange and myrtle boughs. High thoughts and scholarly creation were never more fitly housed than here. Their grounds, covered with trees, plants, fruits and flowers, were then known as the Selva dei

* Since this was written, one-half of these gardens have been destroyed; the other half bought by the Marchese Ginori.

160

Rucellai, and must have been of much larger extent in the time of Machiavelli than they had become even in the eighteenth century; for when Palla Rucellai fled in fear of being compromised in the general hatred of all the Medici followers and friends, he left the Selva by a little postern door in its western wall which opened on to the Porta Prato and the great meadow then surrounding that gateway. Therefore they must then have covered all the space now occupied by the detestable modern streets called Magenta, Solferino, Montebello, Garibaldi, etc., and I have myself indeed conversed with persons who remember, in their youth, the orchards appertaining to these gardens existing where there are now the ugly boulevards and the dirt and lumber of the railway and tramway works.

On this unfortunate flight of Palla in 1527, the populace broke into the gardens, and destroyed the statues, obelisks and temples which ornamented them, but the woods and orchards they appear to have spared; for, some thirty years later, the park seems to have been in its full perfection still, when Ferdinand, in the height of a violent and devoted passion, gave it to his Venetian mistress as her *casin de piacere*, and Bianca brought a mode of life very unlike that of the grave and scholarly Rucellai into its classic groves; for although her fate was tragic, and her mind must have been ever apprehensive of foul play, she was evidently of a gay, mirthful, pleasure-loving temperament.

The jests and pranks, the sports and pastimes, the conjuring and comedy, the mirth and music, the dances and mummeries, which pleased the taste of

Bianca and her women, replaced the 'noble sessions
of free thought' and the illustrious fellowship of the
Academicians. The gravity and decorum of the
philosophical society departed, but the floral and
sylvan beauty remained. At the time when she
filled its glades with laughter and song and the
beauty of her women, the Selva was what was even
then called an English garden, with dense woods,
wide lawns, deep shade, and mighty trees which
towered to the skies. But when it passed into the
hands of Giancarlo de' Medici that Cardinal decorated it with a grotto, a giant, and other *gentilezze*,
and changed it into an Italian garden, with many
sculptural and architectural wonders, and plants and
flowers from foreign countries, employing in his
designs Antonio Novelli, who, amongst other feats,
brought water to it from the Pitti, and built up an
artificial mountain in its midst. He must have done
much to disfigure it, more than the mob of 1527 had
done; but soon after these ill-considered works were
completed the gardens passed to the Ridolfi, who,
preserving the rare flowers and fruits, with which the
Cardinal had planted it, allowed the woodland growth
to return to its freedom and luxuriance. Of him who
ultimately restricted the park to its present limits, and
robbed the house of all its treasures of art and admirable ornament, there is, I believe, no record. From
the Ridolfi it went to a family of Ferrara, of the
name of Canonici, and from them to the Stiozzi, who
sold it in our own time to Prince Orloff, by whose
heir it has once more been put up for sale. Amidst
all these changes the beauty of the park, though
impaired, has existed much as it was when it was

celebrated in Latin and Italian prose and verse,
although diminished in size and shorn of its grandeur,
invaded on all sides by bricks and mortar, and cruelly
violated, even in its inmost precincts. The house has
been miserably modernised, and the gardens and
glades miserably lopped, yet still there is much left ;
and many of their historic trees still lift their royal
heads to morning dawn and evening stars. Enough
remains to make a green oasis in the desert of modern
bricks and stucco ; enough remains for the student
to realise that he stands beneath boughs of cedar
and ilex which once sheltered the august brows of
Leone X. and cast their shade on the gathered
associates of that literary society of which no equal
has ever since been seen. The gardens, even in
their shrunken and contracted space and verdure,
are still there, priceless in memories and invaluable
to the artist, the student and the lover of nature
and of history.

It seems scarcely credible, yet such is the fact, that
these treasures of natural beauty and storehouses of
historical association should have already once been
invaded to build the ordinary modern house called
Palazzo Sonnino, and that now the municipality is
about to purchase half of them—for what purpose?
—*to cut the trees down and cover the ground with
houses for the use of its own office-holders,* those
multitudinous and pestilent *impiegati* who are the
curse of the public all over Italy, and feed on it like
leeches upon flesh. That the destruction of such
gardens as these for such a purpose can even be for
an instant spoken of is proof enough of the depths of
degradation to which public indifference and muni-

cipal vandalism have sunk in the city of Lorenzo. It can only be equalled by the destruction of the Far- nesina and Ludovisi gardens. Few places on earth have such intellectual memories as the Oricellari gardens ; yet these are disregarded as nought, and the cedars and elms which shaded the steps of philosophers and poets, of scholarly princes and mighty Popes, are to be felled, as though they were of no more value than worm-eaten mill-posts.

That a people can be *en masse* so utterly dead to memory, to greatness, to beauty, and to sense, makes any serious thinker despair of its future. There are waste grounds (grounds already deliberately laid waste) yawning by scores already, in the town and around it, on which any new buildings which may be deemed necessary might be raised. There is not one thread or shadow of excuse for the abominable action now contemplated by the Florence Municipality, and certain to be consummated unless some opposition, strong and resolute, arise. Even were the Orti Oricellari a mere ordinary park, without tradition, without heritage, without association, it would be imbecility to cover the site with bricks and mortar, for Maxime du Camp has justly written that whoever fells a tree in a city commits a crime. ' Chaque fois qu'un arbre tombe dans une ville trop peuplée cela équivaut à un meurtre et parfois à une épidémie. On a beau multiplier les squares, ils ne remplaceront jamais la ceinture de forêt qui devrait entourer toute capitale et lui verser l'oxygène, la force, et la santé.' These are words salutary and true, which would be well inscribed in letters of gold above the council chamber of every municipality. When towns are desperately pinched for space, hemmed in on every side, and at their wits' end for lodging-room, there may be some kind of credible excuse for the always mistaken destruction of gardens, trees and groves. But in all the cities of Italy there is no such excuse ; there are vast unoccupied lands all around them ; and in their midst more, many more, houses than are occupied. In Rome and Florence the latter may be counted by many thousands. There is not the feeblest, flimsiest pretext for such execrable destruction as has already overtaken so many noble gardens in the former city, and now menaces the Orti Oricellari in the latter.

Nor is this Selva, although the most famous, the only garden which is being destroyed in Florence, whilst many beautiful glades and lawns have been, in the last ten years, ruthlessly ruined and effaced that the wretched and trumpery structures of the jerry-builders may arise in their stead. The Riccardi garden in Valfonda was once like that of the Oricellari, a marvel of loveliness ; and its lawns, its avenues, its marbles, its deep, impenetrable shades, its sunlit orange-walks and perfumed pergolate, surrounded a house which was a temple of art and contained many choice statues of ancient and contemporary masters. Talleyrand once said that no one who had not lived before the great revolution could ever know how perfect life could be. I would say that none can know how perfect it can be who did not live in the Italy of the Renaissance. Take the life of this one man, Riccardo, Marchese Riccardi, who spent most of his existence in this exquisite pleasure-place, which he inherited from its creator, the great scholar and

dilettante, Romolo Riccardi, and where he resided
nearly all the year round.   In the contemporary
works of Cinelli on the *Bellezze di Firenze*, his house
and gardens are described ; they are alluded to by
Redi,—

> ' Nel bel giardino
> Nei bassi di gualfondo inabissato
> Dove tieni il Riccardi alto domino.'

They are spoken of in admiration by Baldinucci, and,
in the description of the festival of Maria de' Medici's
marriage by proxy to Henri Quatre, they are enthusi-
astically praised by the younger Buonarotti.   The
court of the Casino was filled with ancient marbles,
busts, statues and inscriptions, Latin and Greek ; the
exterior was decorated in fresco and tempera, with
many rare sculptures and paintings and objects of art,
whilst, without, a number of avenues led in all direc-
tions from the house to the gardens and the woods,
where, in shade of ilex and cypress, marble seats and
marble statues gave a sense of refreshing coolness in
the hottest noon.   Here this elegant scholar and
accomplished noble passed almost all his time, receiving all that was most learned and illustrious in the
society of his epoch ; and occasionally giving magnificent entertainments like that with which he bade
farewell to Maria de' Medici.   Of this delicious retreat
a few trees alone remain now ; a few trees, which
raise their sorrowful heads amongst the bricks and
mortar, the theatres and photographic studios, around
them, are all that are left of the once beautiful and
poetic retreat of the scholars and courtiers, the
ambassadors and *illuminati*, of the family of the
Riccardi.   Why has not such a place as this once

was been religiously preserved through all time, for the joy, health and beauty of the city?

It would be scarcely possible for so beautiful and precious a life as this of the Riccardi to be led in our times, because it is scarcely possible, lock our gates as we may, to escape from the detestable atmosphere of excitation and worry which is everywhere around. The mania of senseless movement is now in the human race, as the saltatory delirium seized on the Neapolitan peasants and hurried them in crowds into the sea.

Riccardo Riccardi living now would be ashamed to dwell the whole year round in his retreat of Valfonda; would waste his time over morning newspapers, cigars and ephemeral telegraphic despatches; would probably spend his money on horse-racing; would send his blackletter folios, his first copies, and his before-letter prints to the hammer, and would make over his classic marbles to the Louvre, the Hermitage, or to his own government. He and his contemporaries had the loveliness of leisure and the wisdom of meditation; they knew that true culture is to be gained in the library, not in the rush of a *pérégrinomanie;* and being great, noble and rich, judged aright that the best gifts given by high position and large fortune are the liberty which they allow for repose, and the power which such repose confers to enjoy reflection and possession. In modern life this faculty is almost wholly lost, and the wit and the fool are shaken together in the vibration of railway trains, and jostled together in the eating-houses of the world, till, if the fool thus obtain a varnish of sharpness, the wit has lost all individuality and grace.

Not long since, I said to an Englishman who has

filled high posts and attained high honours, whilst public life is always repugnant to his tastes and temperament, that he would have been wiser to have led his own life in his own way, under his own ancestral roof-tree in England ; and he answered, ' I would willingly have done so, but they would have said that I had nothing in me ! ' Characteristic nineteenth century reply ! Romolo and Riccardo Riccardi did not trouble themselves in their different generations what their contemporaries thought of them. They led their own lives in their own leafy solitude, and only called their world about them when they were themselves disposed to entertain it.

The gardens of the Gaddi were equally and still earlier renowned, and in them the descendants of Taddeo Gaddi had a pleasure-house wondrous and lovely to behold, while the rich gallery of pictures annexed to it was situated next to the Valfonda, and covered what is now the new Piazza di S. M. Novello. These descendants had become great people and eminent in the church, many cardinals and monsignori amongst them, and also celebrated *letterati*, of whom Niccolo, son of Senibaldo, was the most illustrious. He, as well as a scholar and patron of letters and arts, was, like the Riccardi, a botanist, and, as may be seen in the pages of Scipione Ammirato, was foremost for his culture of sweet herbs and of lemons and citrons. Whilst he filled worthily the post of ambassador and of collector of works of art for the Medici, he never forgot his garden and his herb-garden, and was the first to make general in Tuscany the Judas-tree, the gooseberry, the strawberry, the Spanish myrtle, the northern fir and other then rare fruits and shrubs. So

fragrant and so fair were his grounds, that the populace always called them, and the vicinity perfumed by
them, Il Paradiso dei Gaddi.   This beautiful retreat
has for centuries been entirely destroyed and forgotten ; and all which is left of the rich collections of
the Gaddi are those thousand manuscript folios which
Francis I. of Austria purchased and gave to the
libraries of Florence, where to this day they remain
and can be read.

The director of the Gaddi gardens bore the delightful
name of Messer Giuseppe Benincasa Fiammingo ; and
a contented life indeed this worthy and accomplished
student must have led, working for such a patron, and
passing the peaceful seasons and fruitful years amidst
the cedar-shadows and the lemon-flower fragrance of
this abode of the Muses and of Flora and Pomona.

We dwell too much upon the strife and storm, the
bloodshed and the internecine feuds of the passed
centuries ; we forget too often the many happy and
useful lives led in them, which were spent untroubled
and consecrated to fair studies and pursuits, and which
let the clangour of battle go by unheard, and mingled
not with camp or court or council.

We forget too often the placid life of Gui Patin
under his cherry trees by the river, or of the Etiennes,
in the learned and happy seclusion of their classic
studies and noble work, even their women speaking
Latin as their daily and most natural tongue ; we only
have ear for the fusillades of the Fronde, or the war-
cries of Valois and Guise.   In like manner we are too
apt only to dwell upon the daggers and poison
powders, the factions and feuds, the conspiracies and
the city riots of the Moyenage and Renaissance, and

forget the many quiet, useful, happy persons clad in doublet and hose, like Messer Benincasa, and the many learned and noble gentlemen clothed in velvet and satin, like Niccolo Gaddi, his master, who passed peacefully from their cradle to their grave.

In the fifteenth century, according to Benedetto Varchi, who himself saw them, there were no less than a hundred and thirty of these magnificent demesnes in the city; and whatever may have been the sins of the earlier and the follies of the later Medici, that family, one and all, loved flowers, woods and lawns, and fostered tenderly 'il gusto del giardinaggio' in their contemporaries. This taste in their descendants has entirely disappeared. They are bored by such of the magnificent gardens of old as still exist in their towns and around their villas; they abandon them without regret, grudging the care of keeping them up, and letting them out to nursery gardeners or to mere peasants whose only thought is, of course, to make profit out of them.

The Latins were at all times celebrated for their beautiful gardens; all classic records and all archæological discoveries prove it. The Romans and the Tuscans, the Venetians and the Lombards, in later mediæval times, inherited this elegant taste, this art, which is twin child itself with Nature; but in our immediate epoch it has vanished; the glorious legacies of it are supported with indifference or done away with without regret. How is this to be explained? I know not unless the reason be that there has come from without a contagion of vulgarity, avarice and bad taste which the Italian temperament has been too weak to resist, and with which it has become saturated and debased. The modern Italian will

throw money away recklessly on the Bourses or at
the gaming-tables; he will spend it frivolously at
foreign baths and fashionable seaports; he will let
himself be ruined by a pack of idle and good-for-
nothing hangers-on whom he has not the courage to
shake off; but he grudges every penny which is required for the maintenance of woodland and garden,
and he will allow his trees to be felled, his myrtles,
bays and laurels to vanish, his fountains to be
choked up by sand or weed, and his lawns to degener-
ate into rough pasture, without shame or remorse.

Almost all these noble gardens enumerated by
Varchi still existed in Florence before 1859. Now
but few remain. Even the Torrigiani gardens (which
for many reasons one would have supposed would
have been kept intact by that family) have been
almost entirely destroyed within the last year, and
the site of them is being rapidly covered with mean
and ugly habitations. The magnificent Capponi
garden, so dear to the blind statesman and scholar,
Gino Capponi, has been more than half broken up
by his heirs. The renowned Serristori garden was
cut in two and shorn of half of its beauty when the
first half of the Via dei Bardi was destroyed. The
Guadagni garden is advertised as building ground.
The Guicciardini gardens are still standing, but as
they and their palace have been given over to amal-
gamated railway companies, the respite accorded to
them will probably be of brief duration. The bead
roll of these devastated pleasure-grounds and
historic groves could be continued in an almost
endless succession of names and memories, and the
immensity of their irreparable loss to the city is

scarcely to be estimated. When we reflect, moreover, that before 1859 the whole of the ground from
the Carraia Bridge westward was pasture and garden
and avenue, where now there are only bricks and
mortar and a network of ugly streets, we shall more
completely comprehend the senseless folly which built
over such green places, or, where it did not build, made
in their stead such barren, dusty, featureless, blank
spaces as the Piazza degli Zuavi and its congeners.

Ubaldino Peruzzi (who has been buried with pomp·
in Santa Croce!) was the chief promoter and leader
of this mania of·demolition. It was at his instiga-
tion that the Ponte alle Grazie and the chapel of
the Alberti were pulled down; that the Tetto dei
Pisani was destroyed to make way for an ugly
bank; that the noble trees at the end of the
Cascine were felled to make way for a gaudy,
gingerbread bust and a hideous guardhouse; that
the beautiful Stations of the Cross leading to San
Miniato al Monte were destroyed to give place
to vulgar eating-houses and trumpery villas; and
that old palaces, old gardens and old churches were
laid waste to create the bald and monotonous quays
called severally the Lung Arno Serristori and
Torrigiani. Peruzzi began, and for many years
directed, the destruction of the beauties of the city,
and only stopped when, having brought the town to
the verge of bankruptcy, funds failed him, and he
retired perforce from municipal office.

But if it may be feared that the good we do does
perish with us, it is certain that the evil we do does
long survive us, and flourishes and multiplies when
we are dust. The lessons which Peruzzi taught his

fellow-citizens in speculation and spoliation will long
remain, whilst his bones crumble beneath a lying
epitaph. His dead hand still directs the scrambling
haste with which the historic centre of the city is
being torn down, in order that glass galleries, brum-
magem shops, miserable statues, and a general reign
of stucco and shoddy, may, as far as in them lies,
bring the Athens of Italy to a level with some third-
rate American township.

Except with a few rare exceptions, Italians are
wholly unable to comprehend the indignation with
which their callousness fills the cultured observer of
every other nationality. Anxiety to get ready-
money, an ignorance of their true interests, and a
babyish love of new things, however vulgar or
barbarous, have completely extinguished, in the
aristocracy and bureaucracy, all sentiment for the
arts and all reverence for their inheritance and
for the beauty of Nature. It would seem as if a
kind of paralysis of all perception had fallen on
the whole nation. A prince of great culture, refinement and reputed taste having occasion this
year to repair his palace, has stuccoed and coloured
it all over a light ochre yellow! A great noble
sold his ancestral gardens last year to a building
company, and his family clapped their hands with
delight as the first ilex trees fell beneath the axe!
To make a *paven* street in Venice, unneeded, incongruous, vulgar, abhorrent to every educated eye and
mind, Byzantine windows, Renaissance doorways,
admirable scrollworks, enchanting façades, marbles,
and mosaics, of hues like the sea-shell and the sea-
mouse, are ruthlessly torn down and pushed out of

sight for ever. Ruskin in vain protests, his tears scorched up by his rage, and both alike powerless. Gregorovius died recently, his last years embittered and tortured by the daily destruction of the Rome so sublime and sacred to him. I remember well the day when the axe was first laid to the immemorial groves of the Farnesina: a barbarous and venal act, done to gratify private spleen and greed, leaving a mere mass of mud and dirt where so late had been the gracious gardens which had seen Raffaelle and Petrarca pace beneath their shade. The Spanish Duke, Ripalda, whose passionate love for his Farnesina was known to all Rome, died of the sorrow and fever brought on by seeing its desecration, died actually of a broken heart. 'I shall not long survive them,' he said to me, the tears standing in his proud eyes, as he looked on the ruin of his avenues and lawns, which had so late been the chief beauty of the Tiber, facing their sponsor and neighbour, the majestic Farnese Palace.

To the student, the artist, the archæologist, to live in Rome now is to suffer inexpressibly every hour, in mind and heart.

Who does not know the piazza of San Giovanni Laterano as it was? The most exquisite scene of earth stretched around the most beautiful basilica of the world! Go there now: the horizon is closed and the landscape effaced, vile modern erections, crowded, paltry, monstrous in their impudence and in their degradation, shut out the green plains, the azure hills, the divine, ethereal distance, and close around the spiritual beauty of the great church, like bow-legged ban-dogs round a stag at bay. The intolerable outrage of it, the inconceivable shame of it, the crass obstinacy and stupidity which make such havoc possible, should fill the dullest soul with indignation. . Yet such things are being done yearly, daily, hourly, ceaselessly, and with impunity all over Italy, and no voice is raised in protest. · Whenever any such voice is raised, it is seldom that of an Italian ; it is that of Ruskin, Story, Yriarte, Taine, Vernon Lee, Augustus Hare, or it is my own, to the begetting of ten thousand enemies, to the receiving of twice ten thousand maledictions.

Nor is it only in the great cities that such ruin is wrought. In every little hamlet, on every hill and plain there is the same process of destruction going on, which I have before compared to the growth of lupus on a human face. Rapidly, in every direction, the beauty, the marvellous, the incomparable, natural, and architectural beauty of the country is being destroyed by crass ignorance and still viler greed.

Along those famous hillsides, which rise above Careggi, there was, until a few months ago, a landmark dear to all the countryside, a line of colossal cypresses which had been planted there by the hand of the Pater Patriæ, Cosimo de' Medici himself. These grand and noble trees were lately sold, with the ground on which they stood, to a native doctor of Florence, who *immediately felled them*. Yet if before this unpardonable action, in looking on the fallen giants, anyone is moved to see the pity of it and curse the stupid greed which set the axe at their sacred trunks, he who does so mourn is never the prince, the noble, the banker, the merchant, the tradesman ; it is some foreign 'painter or scholar, or some peasant of the soil who remembers the time when one vast avenue connected Florence and Prato.

Within one mile of each other there are, near Florence, a green knoll, crowned with an ancient church, and a river, shaded by poplar trees ; the beauty of the hill was an historic tower, dating from the year 1000, massive, mighty, very strong, having withstood the wars of eight centuries; at its foot was a stately and aged stone pine. The beauty of the river was a wide bend, where the trees and the hills opened out from the water, and a graceful wooden bridge spanned it, chiefly used by the millers' carts and the peasants' mules. In the gracious spring-time of last year, the old tower was pulled down to be used for building materials, for which it was found that it could not be used, and the stone pine was felled, because its shade prevented a few beans to the value of, perhaps, two francs growing beneath it. On the river the white wooden bridge has been pulled down, and a huge, red, brick structure, like a ponderous railway bridge, hideous, grotesque, and shutting out all the sylvan view up stream, has been erected in its stead, altogether unfitted for the slender rural traffic which alone passes there, and costing a heavy price, levied by taxation from a rural, and far from rich, community. Thus are two exquisite landscapes wantonly ruined ; no one who has known those scenes, as they were a year ago, can endure to look at them as they are. There was no plea or pretext of necessity for such a change ; the one was due to private greed, the other to municipal brutishness and speculation; some persons are a few pounds the heavier in purse, the country is for ever so much the poorer.

There is, within another mile, an old castellated villa with two mighty towers, one at either end, and within it chambers panelled with oak carvings of the Quattro Cento, of great delicacy and vigour of execution; it stands amidst a rich champagne country, abounding in vine and grain and fruits, and bears one of the greatest names of history. *It is now about to be turned into a candle manufactory !* In vain do the agriculturists around protest that the filthy stench of the offal which will be brought there, and the noxious fumes of the smoke, which will pour from the furnace chimney about to be erected amongst its fir-trees, will do infinite harm to the vineyards and orchards around. No one gives ear to their lament. Private cupidity and communal greed run hand in hand; and the noble building is doomed beyond hope. Who can hold their soul in patience or seal their lips to silence before such impiety and imbecility as this?

When this kind of destruction is going on everywhere, in every city, town, village, province, commune, all over Italy, who can measure the ultimate effects upon the face of the country? What, in ten years' time, will be left of it as Eustace and Stendahl saw it? What, in twenty years' time, will be left of it as we now know it? Every day some architectural beauty, some noble avenue, some court or loggia or gateway, some green lawn, or shadowy ilex grove, or sculptured basin, musical with falling water, and veiled with moss and maidenhair, is swept away for ever

M

that some jerry-builder may raise his rotten walls or some tradesman put up his plate-glass front, or some dreary desert of rubble and stones delight the eyes of wise modernity.

It is impossible to imagine any kind of building more commonplace, more ugly, and less suitable to the climate than the modern architecture, or rather masons' work, which has become dear to the modern Italian mind. It is the kind of house which was built in London twenty or thirty years ago, and now in London is despised and detested. The fine old hospital of Santa Lucia, strong as a rock, and sound as an oak, has recently been knocked down by a man who, returning with a fortune made in America, desired to be able to name a street after himself. (Streets used to be named after heroes who dwelt in them ; they are now named after *rastaqouères*, who pull them down and build them up again.) Instead of the hospital, there are erected some houses on the model of London houses of thirty years ago, with narrow, ignoble windows and façades of the genuine Bayswater and Westbourne Grove type. There has not been one opposing voice to their erection, and any censure of them is immediately answered by a reference to the brand-new dollars of their builder. In the suburbs it is the hideous cottage (here called *villino*), which, having disgraced the environs of London and Paris, is now rapturously set up in the neighbourhood of Italian towns. Both these types of house-building (for architecture it is absurd to call it) are as degraded as they can possibly be ; and, whereas the London and Paris suburban cottages have frequently the redeeming feature of long windows down

to the ground, modern Italian houses have narrow
windows of the meanest possible kind, affording no
light in winter and no air in summer.   The horrible
English fashion of putting a window on each side of
a narrow doorway is considered beautiful in Italy, and
slavishly followed everywhere, whilst the climbing
roses and evergreen creepers which in England and
France so constantly cover the poorness of modern
houses, are, in Italy, only conspicuous by their absence.
The noble loggias, and balconies, and colonnades of
old Italian mansions were in the old time run over
with the tea rose, the glycine and the banksia ; but
the wretched modern Italian 'villino' is, in all its
impudence, naked and not ashamed.

These dreadful modern constructions, with flimsy
walls, slate roof, pinched doorway, mean windows,
commonness, cheapness and meanness staring from
every brick in their body, are disgracing the approach
of every Italian city ; they are met with climbing the
slope of Bellosguardo, beside the hoary walls of Signa,
behind the cypresses of the Poggio Imperiale, on the
road to the Ponte Nomentana, outside the Porta
Salara, on the way to the baths of Caracalla, close
against the walls of the Colosseum, above the green
canal water of Venice, in front of the glad blue sea by
Santa Lucia, anywhere, everywhere, insulting the past,
making hideous the present, suited to no season and
absurd in every climate, the rickety offspring of a
century incapable of artistic procreation.

It is impossible to enter into the minds of men who
actually consider it a finer thing, a prouder thing, to
be a third-rate, mediocre, commercial city than to be
the first artistic, or the noblest historic, city of the

world. Yet this is what the modern Italian, the Italian who governs in ministry, bureaucracy, municipality, and press, deliberately does prefer. He thinks it more glorious, and worthier, to be a feeble imitation of a shoddy American city than to be supreme in historic, artistic and natural beauty. He will sell his Tiziano, his Donatello, his Greek and Roman marbles, and his Renaissance tapestries without shame; and he will pant and puff with pride because he has secured a dirty tramway coaling-yard, has befouled his atmosphere with mephitic vapours and coaltar gas, and has reduced his lovely *verzaja*, so late green with glancing foliage and fresh with rippling water, into a howling desert of iron rails, shot rubbish, bricks and mortar, unsightly sheds, and smoke-belching chimneys. To the educated observer the choice is as piteous and as grotesque as that of the South Sea Islander greedily exchanging his pure, pear-shaped, virgin pearl for the glass and pinchbeck of a Birmingham brooch.

Not many years ago there was in these gardens of the Oricellari of which I have spoken a neglected statue lying unnoticed in a darksome place. It was the Cupid of Michaelangelo, which, being discovered by the sculptor Santerelli, there and then was sold to the South Kensington Museum, where it may be seen to-day. This will ere long be the fate of all the sculptures and statues of Italy, and the 'modern spirit' now prevailing in the country will consider it best that it should be so.

The empty word of 'progress' which is repeated by all nations in this day, as if they were parrots, and has as much meaning in it as if it were only 'poor poll,' is continually used to cover, or feign to excuse, all these barbarous enormities; but most insincerely, most vainly. To turn a rich agricultural country into a fourth-rate manufacturing one can claim neither sagacity nor prudence as its defence. To demolish noble, ancient and beautiful things, in order to reproduce the modern mushroom-growths of a dreary and dusty 'western township,' can allege neither sense nor shrewdness as its excuse; it is simply extremely silly; even if inspired by greed it is both silly and short-sighted. Yet it is the only thing which the Italian municipal councils consider it excellent to do; they have, after their manner, sufficiently paid tribute to the arts when they have chipped a Luca Della Robbia medallion out of an ancient wall and put it away in a glass case in some gallery, or when they have taken an altar (as they have just taken the silver altar out of San Giovanni) and locked it up in some museum where nobody goes.*

To the arguments of common sense that an altar is as safe, and as visible, in the baptistery as in a museum, and that five centuries have passed over Luca's out-of-door work without wind or weather, heat or frost, impairing it in the least, no one in the municipal council of any town would for a moment attend. They do not want reason or fitness; they only want the vaporous, fussy, greedy, braggart 'modern tone.'

Everyone who has visited Florence knows the house fronting the gate of San Pier Gattolino (Porta Romana), on the front of which are found remnants

* This altar has been since, at the entreaty of the people, replaced in San Giovanni.

of an almost wholly damaged fresco, through which a window has been cut. The house was once radiant with the frescoes of Giovanni di San Giovanni, which Cosimo dé Medici caused to be painted on its façade, because fronting the gateway by which all travellers came from Rome, ' it was to be desired, for the honour of the city, that the first impression of all such travellers should be one of joy and beauty, to the end that such strangers might receive pleasure therein and tarry willingly.' This wise and hospitable reasoning has been utterly lost sight of by those who rule our modern cities, and the approaches to all of them are defiled and disfigured, so that the heart of the traveller sinks within his breast. Instead of Cosimo's gay and gracious fresco-pageantry upon the walls, there are only now, by the Romano gate, a steam tramway belching filthy smoke, a string of carts waiting to be taxed, and a masons' scaffolding where lately towered the Torrigiani trees !

Reflect for a moment what the rule of—we will not say an Augustus, but merely of a Magnifico, of a Francois Premier—might have made in these thirty years of modern Italy. Marvellous beauty, incomparable grandeur of form, surpassing loveliness of Nature, entire sympathy of the cultured world and splendour immeasurable of tradition and example, all these after the peace of Villafranca, as after the breach of Porta Pia, lay ready to the hand of any ruler of the land who could have comprehended their meaning and their magnificence, their assured opportunity and their offered harmony.

But there was no one ; and the moment has long passed.

The country has been guided instead into the
trumpery and ephemeral triumphs of what is called
modern civilisation, and an endless expenditure has
gone hand in hand with a mistaken policy.

Whenever a royal visit is made to any Italian town,
the preparations for it invariably include some frightful act of demolition, as when at Bologna, on the
occasion of the late state visit of the sovereigns, the
noble Communal Palace of that city was bedaubed
all over with a light colouring, and its exquisitely
picturesque and irregular casements were altered,
enlarged, and cut about into the mathematical
monotony dear to the municipal mind, no one present
having sense to see that all the harmony and dignity
of its architecture were ruthlessly obliterated.   Some
similar action is considered necessary in every town,
big or little, before the reception of any prince, native
or foreign.   The results are easily conceived.   It is
said that William of Germany did not conceal his
ridicule of the colossal equestrian statues in *pasteboard*
which were set up in the station entrance at Rome in
his honour; but as a rule the royal persons in Europe
appear not to have any artistic feeling to offend.   The
only two who had any were hurled in their youth, by
a tragic fate, out of a world with which they had little
affinity.   Those who remain have no sympathy for
tradition or for the arts.   The abominations done
daily in their names and before their eyes leave them
wholly unmoved.   Nay, it is no secret that they do
constantly approve and urge on the vandalism of
their epoch.

The Italian people would have been easily led into
a higher and wiser form of life.   (I speak of the Italian

people as distinguished from the Italian bureaucracy and borghesia, which are both of a crass and hopeless philistinism.) The country people especially have an artistic sense still latent in them, and they remain often artistic in their attire, despite the debasing temptations of cheap and vulgar modern clothing. Their ear for music is generally perfect, they detect instantly the false note or the faulty chord which many an educated hearer might let pass unnoticed. Their national songs, serenades, and poems are admirable in purity and grace, and although now, alas! comparatively rarely heard on hillside and by seashore, they remain essentially the verse of the people. Unfortunately this part of the nation is absolutely unrepresented. The noisy agitator, the greedy office-seeker, the unscrupulous politician, the pert, unhealthy lawyer crowd to the front and screech and roar until they are esteemed both at home and abroad to be the sole and indivisible 'public,' whilst their influence, by intrigue and bustle, does most unhappily predominate in all spheres municipal and political; and the entire press, subsidised by them, justifies them in all they do and pushes their selfish and soulless speculations down the throats of unwilling and helpless men.

'Mi son meco,' says Benedetto Varchi, 'molte volte stranamente maravigliato com' esser posso che in quelli uomini i quali son usati per piccolissimo prezzo, insino della prima fanciullezza loro, a portare le balle della Lana in guisi di facchini, e le sporte della Seta a uso di zanaiuoli, ed in somma a star poco meno che schiavi tutto il giorno, e gran pezza della notte alla Caviglia e al fuso, si ritrovi poi in molti di loro, dove e quando bisogna, tanta grandezza d'anima e così nobili e alti pensieri, che sappiamo, e osino non solo di dire ma di fare quelle tante e sì belle cose, ch' eglino parte dicono, e parte fanno.' *

A people of whom this was essentially, and not merely rhetorically, true, would have been with little difficulty kept within the fair realm of art and guided to a fine ideal, in lieu of being given for their guides the purchased quill-men of a venal journalism, and bidden to worship a dirty traction-engine, a plate-glass shop front, and a bridge of cast-iron, painted red.

If through the last thirty years a sovereign with the cultured tastes of a Leonello d'Este or a Lorenzo del Moro, had been dominant in the councils of Italy, he would have made his influence and his desires so felt that the municipalities and ministries would not have dared to commit the atrocities they have done. Constitutional monarchs may be powerless in politics, but in art and taste their power for good and for evil is vast. Alas! in no country in Europe is any one of them a scholar or a connossieur. They have no knowledge of the one field in which alone their influence would be unhampered, and might be salutary. They think themselves forced to pat and

* 'I have in myself wondered strangely many a time how it is possible that in men who from their earliest youth have been used at the lowest price to bear bales of wool as porters and baskets of silk as carriers, and in a word to be little better than slaves all the day long, and to spend a great part of the night at carding and spinning, can in so many cases display, when there is opportunity and need, so much greatness of soul and such high and noble thoughts, and cannot only say but do such beautiful things as are said and done by them.'

Zanaiuoli means, literally, 'whoever carries a basket'; there is no exact English equivalent.

praise the modern playthings of war and science, and of beauty they have no conception, of antiquity they have merely jealousy.

It is to be deplored, not only as a national, but as a world-wide, loss that Modern Italy has entirely missed and misconceived the way to true greatness and to true prosperity. In other centuries she was the light of the world ; in this she deliberately prefers to be the valet of Germany and the ape of America. Had there been men capable of comprehending her true way to a new life, and capable of leading her varied populations in that way, she might have seen a true and a second Renaissance. But those men are not existing, have not existed, within recent times for her ; her chiefs have all been men who, on the contrary, knew nothing of art and cared nothing for nature ; a statesman like Cavour, a conspirator like Mazzini, a free-lance like Garibaldi, a soldier like Victor Emmanuel were none of them men to understand, much less to re-create, the true genius of the nation; their eyes were fixed on political troubles, on social questions, on acquisition of territory, on quarrels with the Pope, and alliances with reigning houses. Since their death lesser people have taken their places, but have all followed in the same tracks, have all misled the nation to imagine that her *risorgimento* lies in copying American steam-engines and keeping ironclads ready for a signal from the potentate of Berlin.

Italy might be now, as she was in the past, the Muse, the Grace, the Artemis and the Athene of the world ; she thinks it a more glorious thing to be only one amongst a sweating mob of mill-hands.

Italy, beautiful, classic, peaceful, wise with the wisdom inherited from her fathers, would have been the garden of the world, the sanctuary of pure art and of high thought, the singer of immortal song. Instead, she has deliberately chosen to be the mere imitator of a coarse and noisy crowd on the other side of the Atlantic, and the mere echo of the armed bully who dictates to her from the banks of the Spree.

L'UOMO FATALE

IF there were any free speech or free action in matters political permitted in what is known as Free Italy, it would be at once interesting and useful to ask of its Government under what *régime* they govern? Is it under a constitutional monarchy, a dictatorship, a military despotism, or what? The reply would probably be that it is still a constitutional monarchy with popular parliamentary representation. But the counter reply would be: Then why are all the restraints limiting a constitutional sovereign broken through and all the privileges appertaining to, and creating the purpose of, parliamentary representation violated or ignored? When the king of a constitutional Italy violated the Constitution in refusing the Zanardelli Cabinet because it did not promise acquiescence in his own views, the country should have protested, and insisted on the Zanardelli Cabinet being placed in power for the sake of the constitutional principle therein involved. It was the first step towards absolutism. If it had been promptly stopped and punished there would have been no more similar steps. It was allowed to pass unchastised, and the result has been that every succeeding week which has since passed has seen worse and continual violations of the Constitution and the Code.

'*L'uomo fatale*,' as the Italian people call Crispi, was summoned to rule, and the result has been, what everyone cognisant of his character knew would be inevitable, namely, the abolition of all liberties and safeguards of the body politic, and the substitution of secret, irresponsible, and absolutely despotic, tribunals, and secret agencies, worked by the will of one man. The revolutionary movement has been crushed by military force with a brutality and injustice which, were the scene Russia or Austria, would cause monster meetings of indignation in London. Led by *The Times*, *The Post*, and other journals, English opinion is deaf and blind to the tyrannies which it would be the first to denounce in any other nation. English opinion does not choose to understand, and does not desire to be forced to understand, that Italy is at the present time as completely ruled by an unscrupulous despotism, and by sheer use of the sabre and musket, as is Poland at this hour, or as Austrian Venetia was earlier in the century; and that Italy presents the same spectacle of prisoners, purely political, being hustled through the towns manacled by handcuffs and chained to one another by a long iron fetter; lawyers, landowners, merchants, editors, men of education, probity and honourable life being yoked with the common criminal and the hired bravo. It is difficult to comprehend how and why this shameful outrage upon decency and liberty is viewed with indifference by the rest of Europe. That it may give pleasure to the foes of Italy is easily understood; but how can it fail to give pain and alarm to her friends? How is it that unanimous protest and unanimous censure do not arise from all those who profess to recognise the necessity of freedom for national well-being?

The extreme gravity of the fact that the Italian sovereign chooses and caresses a minister who is permitted to set aside at will all ordinary provisions and protections of the law, does not appear to excite any astonishment or apprehension outside Italy. In Italy itself the people are paralysed with fear; the steel is at their throats, and the army, which they have been ruined to construct and maintain, crushes them into silence and exhaustion.

Let the English people picture to themselves what would have been the verdict of Europe if England had dealt with Ireland as Sicily has been dealt with; let them imagine Lord Wolseley acting like General Morra; let them imagine a cordon drawn around the whole island, ingress and egress forbidden under pain of arrest, telegrams destroyed, approaching vessels fired upon, the whole population forcibly disarmed, no news—save such as might be garbled by superior order—permitted to be despatched from the interior to the world at large, thousands of men thrust into prison on suspicion whilst their families starved, absolute secrecy, absolute darkness and mystery covering irresponsible despotism; let the English public imagine such a state as this in Ireland, and then ask themselves what would be the verdict of Europe and America upon it. Sicily contains two millions of persons, and this vast number has been given over to the absoulte will of a single brutal soldier, who is screened by ministerial protection from any ray of that daylight of publicity which is the only guarantee for the equity of public men.

We are told that the island is pacified. So is a garotted and blindfolded creature pacified; so is a murdered corpse pacified. The most merciless reprisals have followed on the attempts of the peasantry to save themselves from the grinding extortions of their usurers and the pitiless taxation of their communes; and the reign of terror which has been established is called tranquillity. The same boast of 'peace when there is no peace' is made in the Lunigiana.

There is not even the gloss of affected legality in the countless arrests which have filled to overflowing the prisons of Italy. The charges by which these arrests are excused are so wide that they are a net into which all fish, big and little, may be swept. The imputation of 'inciting to hatred between the classes' is so vague that it may include almost any expression of social or political opinion. It is an accusation under which almost every great writer, thinker or philosopher would be liable to arrest, and under which Jesus Christ and Jean Jacques Rousseau, Garibaldi and John Milton, Washington and Brahma, Tolstoi and St Paul would be all alike condemned as criminals.

Equally vague is the companion accusation of inciting to civil war. As I pointed out in my article of last month, Italy owes her present existence entirely to civil war. Civil war may be a dread calamity, but it may be also an heroic remedy for ills far greater than itself. What is called authority in Italy is so corrupt in itself that it cannot command the respect

of men, and has no title to demand their obedience.
The creator itself of civil war and disturbance, such
authority becomes ridiculous when draping itself in
the toga of an intangible dignity. Moreover, it is
now incarnated in the person of a single unscrupulous
opportunist. Why should the nation respect either
his name or his measures ? The King of Italy, always
servilely copying Germany, has decreed the name and
measures of the lawyer Crispi sacred, as Germany
has sent to prison many writers and printers for having expressed opinions hostile to the acts or speeches
of German public men. Under the state called *piccolo
stato d'assedio* military tribunals judge civil offences,
or what are considered offences, and pass sentences of
imprisonment varying in duration from six months to
thirty years. The infamous sentence of twenty-three
years' imprisonment, of which three are to be passed
in solitary confinement, passed on the young advocate
Molinari, for what is really no more than an offence
of opinions, has forced a cry of surprise and disgust
even from the German press. The monstrous iniquity
of this condemnation has made even the blind and
timid worm of Italian public feeling turn writhing
under the iron heel which is crushing it, and this
individual sentence is to be carried for appeal into
the civil courts, where it is fervently to be hoped it
may be altered if not cancelled.* Hundreds of
brutal sentences have been passed for which there is
no hope or chance of appeal, and vast numbers of
men, in the flower of youth or the prime of manhood,
are being flung into the hell of Italian prisons, there

* It was not cancelled, and Molinari is now in the *ergustolo* of
Oneglia.

to be left to rot away in unseen and unpitied suffering, till death releases them or insanity seizes them. Insanity comes quickly in such torture as Italian prison-life is to its victims.

A journal called *L'Italia del Popolo* contained a spirited and eloquent article proving that Crispi was neither courageous nor honest, as a Socialist deputy had in a moment of flattery called him : this perfectly legitimate and temperate article caused the confiscation of the paper! 'If Crispi be Almighty God, let us know it!' said the *Secolo* of Milan, a courageous and well-written daily newspaper which has itself been frequently confiscated for telling the truth.

As specimens of other sentences passed in the month of February of the present year, take the following examples :

In Siena the proprietor of the journal *Martinello del Calle* was condemned to thirty-five days of prison for having called the deputy Piccarti 'violent and grotesque.'

The journal *Italia del Popolo* was seized because it contained quotations from the Memoirs of Kossuth.

The *Secolo* of Milan was seized for protesting against the condemnation to *twenty years'* imprisonment of the soldier Lombardino, although he had completely proved his innocence of the offence attributed to him.

The barber, Vittorio Catani, having been heard, in the Piazza S. Spirito of Florence, to say that the revolts in Sicily were due to hunger and distress, was condemned to three months' imprisonment and fifty francs fine.

At San Giuseppe, in Sicily, an old peasant sur-

N

rendered one gun ; confessed to having a better one, and showed where he had put it ; he was sentenced to a year's imprisonment.

A day-labourer, Stefano Grosso, went to visit his father who was dying; a revolver being found in the cottage, during his visit, he was condemned to six months of prison for owning it, although there was no proof of his ownership.

The brothers Di Gesù, herdsmen, accustomed to sleep in a building where many other persons slept also, were sentenced to a year and a half of prison because an old rusty gun, quite useless, was found in a cupboard, although there was no evidence whatever that they owned, or knew of its existence.

These are a few typical instances of sentences passed by the hundred, and tens of hundreds, at the present hour in the unhappy kingdom of Italy. Everyone suspected however slightly, accused however indirectly, is arrested and removed from sight. Oftentimes, as in Molinari's case, the sentence embraces periods of solitary confinement, that infernal mental torture under which the strongest intellect gives way. What is the rest of Europe about that it views unmoved such suffering and such tyranny as this ? Let it be remembered that the vast majority of these prisoners have no crime at all on their consciences. Molinari, sentenced in his youth to twenty-three years of prison, has committed no sin except that of being a Socialist. The term Anarchist is constantly used by the tribunals to describe men who are merely guilty of such opinions as are held by your Fabian Society in England.

There has been no actual *coup d'état*, but there has

been what is worse, because less tangible, than a *coup
d'état*, namely, the insidious and secretive alteration of
a constitutional Government into a despotic one, the
unauthorised and illegitimate suppression of free
discussion and of lawful measures, and the substitution for them of arbitrary methods and secret-police
investigation. The change has been quite as great
as that which was wrought in Paris by the canon of
the Tenth of December, but it has been made by
means more criminal, because less open and as yet
unavowed. The King of Italy, having mounted the
throne under an engagement to hold inviolate the
Constitution, has violated it as violently as Louis
Napoleon his oath to the French Republic ; but he
has done so more insidiously and less courageously,
having never dared to announce to his people his
intention to do so. His decree postponing the
assembling of the Chambers because ' public discussion would be prejudicial' was a virtual declaration
that parliamentary government was at an end, but
the fact was covered by an euphemism. In like
manner, Crispi has said that he will 'ask' for irresponsible powers to be given him, but he defers the
day of asking, and *ad interim* takes those powers
and uses them as he chooses. The Italian Chambers
are to be allowed to meet, but it is intimated to
them that unless they vote for the 'full powers'
they will be dissolved, and a more obedient Parliament elected under the military law of the existing reign of terror. 'La camera sapra quelle che
si deve sapere,' Crispi stated the other day ; that
is, he will tell them as much as he chooses them
to know. The amount of the financial deficit is

to be put before the Chambers as one half only of
what it really is. If there be any exposure made, or
hostility shown, he has his weapon ready to his hand
in dissolution. A new chamber elected under his
docile prefects and his serried bayonets will not fail
to be the humble spaniel he requires. If the present
deputies, when the decree proroguing their assembly
was proclaimed, had all met in Rome, and, without
distinction of party or group, had insisted on the
opening of Parliament, and compelled the monarch to
keep his engagement to the Constitution, it is possible that both he and his minister would have sub-
mitted. But Italian deputies are poor creatures, and
the few men of mark and strength who are amongst
them are swamped under the weight of the inverte-
brate numbers. Hence we are scandalised by the
spectacle of a whole body of the elected representatives of a nation being muzzled and set aside, and
their discussion of opinion and action declared prejudicial to the interests of their country. It would be
simpler and more candid to sweep away Parliament
and Senate altogether than to make of them a mere
mechanical dummy, pushed aside as useless lumber
whenever there is any agitation or danger before
their country. Umberto of Savoia would hesitate to
proclaim himself an absolute sovereign, but *de facto*,
though not *de jure*, he has made himself one. The
text of the Treaty of the Triplice has never been
made known to the country. Rumours have been
heard that there are private riders attached to it
which personally bind the House of Savoy to the
House of Hohenzollern, and cause the otherwise inexplicable, and in every event culpable, obstinacy ●f

the Italian sovereign in insisting on the inviolability of the military *cadres*. Be this as it may, the engagements of the treaty are kept a profound secret, and such secrecy is probably one of the clauses. Now, if the will and signature of one man suffice to pledge a nation in the dark to the most perilous obligations none can predict the issue, what is this except an absolute monarchy? What pretence can there still be of a constitutional Government?

Let the English nation figure to itself their Queen binding them secretly to the most onerous engagements which might cause in the end the total exhaustion and even extinction of their country, and they will then comprehend what Italians are enduring, and have long endured, from the secret pact of their sovereign, of which they have no means to measure the dangers or the responsibilities, although the burden and terror of these lie upon them. It is only by means of the military gag that the sovereign can keep mute the popular anxiety, curiosity and alarm.

The only reforms which would be of the slightest practical use would be the abolition of the hated gate-tax, and salt-tax,* and the reduction of the military and naval expenditure. There is no ministry of any party who dares propose these, the only possible, alleviations of the national suffering.

The formation of the Kingdom of Italy has been aggrandisement, gain and rejoicing to the Piedmontese and Lombard States, but it has been only

* To such an extent is the espionage on the salt-tax carried that a poor man living on the seashore is not allowed to take up more than one pail of sea-water to his house in one day lest he should expose the water to the heat of the sun and use the few salt crystals which its evaporation would leave at the bottom of the pail.

oppression, loss and pain to the country south of the Appenines. Even in the Veneto, if the gauge of felicity be prosperity, the province must miserably regret the issue of its longed-for liberation. ' Piû gran' miseria non c'è sulla terra che n' l'è la nostra,' says a gondolier of Venice to me in this ninety-fourth year of the century. The magnificent and hardy race of gondoliers is slowly and wretchedly perishing, under the grinding wheels of communal extortion, and the ignoble rivalry of the dirty steamboats and the electric launches. But there is greater misery still than theirs, such misery as makes the worst hell of Dante's heaven by comparison—the misery of the children in Sicily, little white slaves sold for a hundred, or a hundred and fifty francs each, to brutal blows, smarting wounds, incessant labour, and absolutely hopeless bondage.

Court-martial is substituted for civil law at the mere will of the monarch and his minister. There has been nothing in the recent events which can justify the establishment of it, and its abominable and irresponsible decrees, in which the torture of solitary confinement so largely figures. Local dissensions and jealousies find vent in accusations and condemnations, and the barbarity of the soldier and the gendarme to the civilian is regarded as a virtue and rewarded. What can be said of a Government which confounds the political writer with the brigand of the hills, the peaceful doctrinaire with the savage assassin, the harmless peasant with the poisoner or strangler, and chains them all together, and pushes them all together into prison-cells, fœtid, pestilent, wretched, already overcrowded? What will be done with all these

thousands? What will be made of all this loss and
waste of life? Miserable as is the existence of Italian
felons, they must eat something, however scanty. The
cost to the country of their useless, stagnant, fettered
lives will be immense, whilst their own anguish will
be unspeakable. Many of them, I repeat, are guilty
of no offence whatever except of desiring a republic,
or professing Socialist doctrines. I have no personal leaning towards Socialism, and regard it as
unworkable, and believe that it would be pernicious
if it could be brought to realisation. But it is no
crime to be a Socialist. Socialism is an opinion, a
doctrine, a creed, an idea ; and those who hold it have
every right to make a propaganda when they can. It
is monstrous that, at the pleasure of a monarch or a
minister, an idea can be treated as a capital crime.
The young advocate Molinari is guilty of nothing
except of inculcating revolutionary doctrines. What
sin is this ? It is one shared by Gautama and Christ.

Maxime du Camp has just died, a member of the
Academy of France. He was once one of the Thousand of Marsala. What is now bringing intellectual
and gifted youths to the felon's dock in Italy is precisely such a creed as drove the late Academician
to enrol himself under Garibaldi. Who shall affirm
that there may not be in these young men, thus in-
famously judged and sentenced to-day, such brilliant
intelligence and critical acumen as have made Maxime
du Camp the admired of all who can appreciate
scholarship, style, perception and true philanthropy,
whether they may or may not agree with his arguments or endorse his deductions ?

It would be impossible for any generous or unselfish

nature not to burn with indignation before the poverty
entailed on Italy by military madness, and the suffering caused to the poor and harmless by the fiscal and
municipal tyrannies and the hired spies and extor-
tioners of the Government.* Jules Simon said the
other day that pity is the mark of great souls. In
Italy it is considered the mark of the malefactor. A
young nobleman of the Lunigiana, Count Lazzoni,
has now a price set upon his head because he has
espoused and taught the doctrines of Mazzini. He
was rich, gifted, fortunate ; his family insisted that he
should give up either his doctrines or themselves, and,
with themselves, his estates and title. He chose to
abandon the last, not without great personal affliction,
because he was tenderly attached to his relatives.
This young hero is now being hunted by soldiery,
and when found will be tried by court-martial under
the convenient charge of 'exciting to class-hatreds.'
Yet what are such young men as these but the very
salt and savour of a country? It is not they who are
the criminals, but the egotists who dance and dine,
and gamble and smoke, and bow at the Quirinale, and
the Vatican, and pay court to the favourites of the
hour, and care nothing what ruin hangs over their
country, nor what suffering is entailed on their countrymen, so long as they get a rosette for their buttonhole,
or rear the favourite for a race in their stables. They
are the true criminals ; not the youths, like Molinari
and Lazzoni, not the men like De Felice and Barbato,
who think and feel and dare.

Why are not the young Princes of the House of

* The taxes of the Government amounted to four hundred millions
odd in 1873 ; in 1893 they amount to over eight hundred millions.

Savoy amongst the suffering peasantry of Sicily, seeing
with their own eyes, hearing with their own ears, doing
something to aid, to mitigate, to console, instead of
spending their lives in leading cotillons, driving
tandem, trying on new uniforms, and shooting in all
seasons of the year? Why do they not go and live
for a month in the sulphur-mines, carry the creels of
sulphur on their bare backs, and feel the stinging
smart of it in their blinded eyes and dried-up throats
and excoriated lips? They would then, at least, know
something of how a portion of their people live and
die. It would be more useful than dressing up in
plumes and armour to amuse William of Prussia.

Lockroy, in writing to the French newspaper
L'Eclair, says that Italy is served well by her public
servants, and possesses unlimited resources and marvellous genius. In what way is she well served by
her public servants? She is stripped bare by all who
pretend to serve her, and everyone who enters her
service, high and low, seeks only to advantage and
enrich himself. Corruption, like dry-rot in a tree, per-
meates the whole public organisation of Italy, from the
highest to the lowest official. All the municipalities
are rotten and rapacious. Nothing is done without
mancia ; or, as it is called further East, *backsheesh.*
The law courts are swarming hotbeds of bribery and
perjury.

Her natural resources may be great, but they are
so burdened by impost and tax, so strained, fettered,
prematurely harvested and spent, that they are ex-
hausted ere they are ripe. Of her genius there is
but little fruit in these days ; there is no originality
in modern Italian talent ; in art, literature, science,

architecture, all is imitation, and imitation of an ignoble model ; the national sense of beauty, once so universal, so intense, is dead ; the national grace and gaiety are dying ; the accursed, withering, dwarfing, deforming spirit of modernity has passed like a blast over the country and made it barren.

In the people there are still beauty of form and attitude, charm and elegance of manner, infinite patience, infinite forbearance, infinite potentialities of excellence as of evil. But they need a saviour, a guide, a friend; they need a Marcus Aurelius, a Nizahualcoytl, a St Louis, a Duke Frederic of Montefeltro, a ruler who would love them, who would raise them, who would give them food bodily and mental, and lead them in the paths of peace and loveliness. Instead of such, what have they? Men who set their wretched ambition on the approving nod of a Margrave of Brandenburg ; who deem it greatness to turn a whole starving peasantry into a vast ill-ordered, ill-equipped, and ill-fed army ; who, for pomp, parade, and windy boast seize the last coin, the last crust, the last shirt ; who find a paltry ideal in an American machine-room, an elevated railway, and an electric gun ; and who deem an ignoble vassalage to the German Emperor meet honour and glory for that Italy which was empress of the earth and goddess of the arts when the German was a forest-brute, a hairy boor, a scarce human Caliban of northern lands.

As events have moved within the last few weeks it is wholly within the bonds of possibility, even of probability, that if the Crown and its chief counsellor see greater danger to themselves threaten them in the coming year, they may appeal for armed help to their ally, who is almost their suzerain, and a fence of Prussian bayonets may be placed around the Quirinale and the House of Assembly. Who shall say that the secret and personal treaty does not provide for such protection?

So far as a public opinion can be said to exist in Italy (for in a French or English sense of the words it does not as yet exist), it is stirring to deep uneasiness and indignation at the subserviency of the tribunals to the ferocity of the Government in what is compared to the Bloody Assize of the English Jeffreys. It is becoming every day more and more alarmed at the absolutism of a King, all criticism of whose acts is made penal, yet whose personal interference and obstruction is every day becoming more obvious, more galling, and more mischievous. A new place of deportation for the condemned of Massa-Carrara is being prepared on the pestilential shore of the Southern Maremma. This new *ergastolo* may prove not only a tomb for those confined in it; but it may very possibly become a pit in which the Italian monarchy will be buried. If the next election should return, as it may do, two hundred of the Extreme Left, '*l'uomo fatale*' may be the cause of a revolution as terrible as that of 1789.

Foreign speakers and writers of the present hour predict the success of Crispi. What is meant by the word? What success is there possible? The enforced acceptance of additional taxation? The placing of the last straw which breaks the camel's back? The quietude which in the body politic, as in the physical body, follows on drainage of the blood and

frequently presages the faintness of death? The
reduction of parliamentary representation to a mere
comedy and formula? The passive endurance of
martial tyranny by a frightened nation, whose terror
is passed off as acquiescence? The increase of debt,
the enlargement of prisons, the paralysis of the public
press?

These are the only things which can be meant by
the success of Francesco Crispi, or can be embodied
in it.

He is the brummagen Sylla of an age of sham, but
he has all the desire of Sylla to slay his enemies and
to rule alone.

In this sense, but only in this sense, he may succeed.
Around the sham Sylla, as around the real Sylla,
there may be laid waste a desolated and silent country,
in which widows will mourn their dead, and fatherless
children weep for hunger under burning roofs. Such
triumph as this he may obtain. Italy has seen many
triumph thus, and has paid for their triumph with her
tears and with her blood.

March 1894.